Climbers rappel into the
Greenland ice sheet.

NATIONAL
GEOGRAPHIC
KiDS

EXTREME PLANET

CARSTEN PETER'S ADVENTURES IN VOLCANOES, CAVES, CANYONS, DESERTS, AND BEYOND!

CARSTEN PETER

WITH GLEN PHELAN

NATIONAL GEOGRAPHIC
WASHINGTON, D.C.

FOR LEO LEANDER
—CARSTEN PETER

STAFF FOR THIS BOOK
Erica Green, *Project Editor*
James Hiscott, Jr., *Art Director/Designer*
Lisa Jewell, *Photo Editor*
Carl Mehler, *Director of Maps*
Sven M. Dolling, Michael McNey, and Mapping
  Specialists, *Map Research and Production*
Paige Towler, *Editorial Assistant*
Rachel Kenny and Sanjida Rashid, *Design
  Production Assistants*
Michael Cassady, *Rights Clearance Specialist*
Grace Hill, *Managing Editor*
Mike O'Connor, *Production Editor*
Lewis R. Bassford, *Production Manager*
Rachel Faulise, *Manager, Production Services*
Susan Borke, *Legal and Business Affairs*
John Chow, *Imaging*

PUBLISHED BY THE NATIONAL GEOGRAPHIC SOCIETY
Gary E. Knell, *President and CEO*
John M. Fahey, *Chairman of the Board*
Melina Gerosa Bellows, *Chief Education Officer*
Declan Moore, *Chief Media Officer*
Hector Sierra, *Senior Vice President and General
  Manager, Book Division*

SENIOR MANAGEMENT/KIDS PUBLISHING AND MEDIA
Nancy Laties Feresten, *Senior Vice President;*
Jennifer Emmett, *Vice President, Editorial Director,
Kids Books;* Julie Vosburgh Agnone, *Vice President,
Editorial Operations;* Rachel Buchholz, *Editor
and Vice President,* NG Kids *magazine;* Michelle
Sullivan, *Vice President, Kids Digital;* Eva Absher-
Schantz, *Design Director;* Jay Sumner, *Photo
Director;* Hannah August, *Marketing Director;*
R. Gary Colbert, *Production Director*

DIGITAL
Anne McCormack, *Director;* Laura Goertzel,
Sara Zeglin, *Producers;* Emma Rigney, *Creative
Producer;* Bianca Bowman, *Assistant Producer;*
Natalie Jones, *Senior Product Manager*

The National Geographic Society is
one of the world's largest nonprofit
scientific and educational organizations. Founded in 1888 to "increase
and diffuse geographic knowledge,"
the Society's mission is to inspire people to care
about the planet. It reaches more than 400 million
people worldwide each month through its official
journal, *National Geographic*, and other magazines;
National Geographic Channel; television documentaries; music; radio; films; books; DVDs; maps;
exhibitions; live events; school publishing programs; interactive media; and merchandise.
National Geographic has funded more than 10,000
scientific research, conservation, and exploration
projects and supports an education program promoting geographic literacy.

For more information, please visit national
geographic.com, call 1-800-NGS LINE (647-5463),
or write to the following address:

National Geographic Society
1145 17th Street N.W.
Washington, D.C. 20036-4688 U.S.A.

Visit us online at nationalgeographic.com/books

For librarians and teachers: ngchildrensbooks.org

More for kids from National Geographic:
kids.nationalgeographic.com

For information about special discounts for bulk
purchases, please contact National Geographic
Books Special Sales: ngspecsales@ngs.org

For rights or permissions inquiries, please contact
National Geographic Books Subsidiary Rights:
ngbookrights@ngs.org

Peter, Carsten, author.
 Extreme planet : Carsten Peter's adventures in volcanoes, caves, canyons, deserts, and beyond! / by
Carsten Peter, with Glen Phelan.
   pages cm
 Audience: Ages 8-12
 Includes bibliographical references and index.
 ISBN 978-1-4263-2100-9 (pbk. : alk. paper) -- ISBN
978-1-4263-2101-6 (library binding : alk. paper)
 1. Peter, Carsten--Juvenile literature. 2. Geology--
Juvenile literature. 3. Extreme environments--
Juvenile literature. 4. Earth (Planet)--Juvenile literature. 5. Nature photography. I. Phelan, Glen,
author. II. National Geographic Society (U.S.) III.
Title. IV. Title: Carsten Peter's adventures in volcanoes, caves, canyons, deserts, and beyond.
 TR140.P45P48 2015
 551--dc23
                                      2015013169

Printed in Hong Kong
15/THK/1

CONTENTS

INTRODUCTION

DID YOU EVER WANT to visit a place so badly that you thought about it day and night? Maybe it was a national park like Yellowstone, an impressive structure like the Eiffel Tower in Paris, or a famous building like the Taj Mahal. Maybe you saw awesome photographs of it and said, "I just have to see this place in person!"

For me, that place was Mount Etna. I loved looking at photos of this active volcano. But I really wanted to see Etna for myself. I bugged my parents for years to go there. Finally, at the age of 15, my dream came true. We took a vacation from our home in southern Germany to the Italian island of Sicily—home of the famous Mount Etna.

A tour bus took us nearly 11,000 feet (3,353 m) to the top of the volcano. I breathed the thin air and walked slowly to the edge of the crater to look inside. It was a steep abyss with sheer vertical walls. Smoke covered the crater floor so it looked bottomless. I couldn't take my eyes off it. I pictured the melted rock boiling beneath and then bursting out in an eruption. I could sense the awesome power. That's when I became obsessed with volcanoes.

Since then I have explored and photographed dozens of volcanoes all around the world—from the rain forests of Indonesia to the scorched plains of Africa to the frigid ice sheets of Antarctica. I've stood within arm's reach of red-hot boiling lava. I've felt the rumble of volcanoes coming to life and then dodged flying chunks of rock during eruptions.

In this book, I'll share with you some of my volcano adventures. You too will sense the awesome power of these forces of nature as we climb inside a crater and stand next to a lake of bubbling lava. But that's not all. I'll share my journeys into the depths of glaciers. Imagine exploring these icy blue masses from the inside! Then we'll warm up quickly as we trek across the world's largest desert—on a camel. We'll make mind-boggling discoveries as we explore caves and canyons. We'll even hunt down forces of nature in the air as we chase tornadoes and lightning across the Great Plains of the United States.

Along the way you'll learn the science behind these extreme places and events. Why do volcanoes form where they do? What causes crystals the size of tree trunks to grow in a cave? What makes narrow slot canyons so dangerous to explore? How is technology helping us learn more and more about tornadoes and lightning? You'll find the answers to these and lots of other questions about our extreme planet.

People often ask me why I do it. Why do I put myself in scary, dangerous situations just to get a photograph? First, it's never *just* a photograph. My photos—and those of other nature photographers—are a way to show people natural wonders they've never seen before. Through our photos, we can share our experiences and our appreciation for the beauty, the mystery, the wonder of our planet. That's a special gift and one I want to pass on.

Another thing that draws me to extreme places is curiosity. When you're riding down a winding road, do you want to know what's around the next bend? I do. When I come upon a cave entrance, I want to know what it's like inside. What will I see, hear, smell, feel? That curiosity drives me to explore and photograph seldom seen (or never before seen) places.

I also enjoy the physical and mental challenge of exploring extreme places and getting just the right photo—that dramatic shot that will stick in your mind. It's not easy. To get unique shots, I have had to become an expert climber, a scuba diver, and even a pilot of a motorized paraglider. I've worked with engineers to invent gadgets that can go places I can't.

All of this hard work has paid off. You'll see amazing photos in this book— some of my favorites, in fact. I hope they spark your imagination and curiosity. Mostly I hope that by sharing my adventures you'll come to appreciate nature—not only extreme places, but also the nature right outside your door. Whether it's a creek, a patch of prairie, a grove of woods, or just a tree on the school grounds, it's there for you to explore. Maybe take a few photos while you're at it.

And now . . . onward to adventure!
Carsten Peter

CHAPTER I

Volcanoes

>>>

[Openings in Earth's crust and the mountains around them from which gases and melted rock spill onto the surface]

Carsten Peter / Mount Semeru, Indonesia

WE WERE LYING ON THE GROUND, STARING AT THE STARLIT SKY.

The night air was cold, but the ground was invitingly warm. We were resting on top of Mount Stromboli, an active volcano! It could erupt at any moment. Were we scared? Not yet.

I was 17 and my friend and I had been looking forward to this adventure for a long time. We had started our climb up the volcano's steep slopes in the late afternoon. For three hours, we struggled and scrambled over the rocky and sandy terrain. Finally we stood atop the mountain. The view of the Mediterranean Sea 3,000 feet (914 m) below us was spectacular. We could even see the nearby coast of the Italian mainland. But the most captivating view was the gaping volcanic crater that lay before us.

Peering into the crater, we looked toward the vent, or opening, in the crater floor about 600 feet (183 m) below. No steam rose from the vent, but the air had a sulfuric, rotten egg smell—a sign that the volcano was alive and well. It was like watching a sleeping giant. And when that giant awakened, I wanted to take its picture. I quickly set up my camera on the tripod that I had lugged up the mountain. In the cold and excitement, I fumbled a bit with the equipment. Finally, I was ready to take my very first photo of a volcanic eruption. Now all I needed was the eruption.

As we rested on the warm ground, I imagined the red-hot magma churning beneath us. What

NIGHT ON STROMBOLI

would it be like, I wondered, to see and feel that molten, gooey rock blast from the crater? I didn't have to wonder for long.

Suddenly, we felt it. A bone-rattling shock wave from deep inside the mountain shook us violently. I sat up and braced myself against the ground. I don't know how long the shaking lasted—maybe only a fraction of a second—but it signaled that magma was rising rapidly inside the volcano. Moments later, the magma burst out of the vent in a fiery fountain. The giant had awakened.

Chunks of partially molten rock—called lava bombs—blasted high into the sky. I'll never forget the sight of those football-size bombs shooting out at rocket speed, slowing into graceful arcs, and hurtling back toward the earth. It would've made for some fantastic photos, but with the glowing fire-like balls above us, we panicked. Terrified, we ran away, as fast as we could, with our backs to one of nature's most dazzling displays. About 100 feet (30 m) from the crater, we did stop to watch, shocked at the forces around us.

The eruption didn't last long, but another one occurred about 20 minutes later. We were no longer startled, and I got some awesome photos. In fact, Stromboli erupted several times that night. The lava bombs flew toward the other side of the crater, so we were never in any real danger. Yet, it was incredible to witness this powerful force up close. It was the first of my many extreme adventures.

The "construction" of Stromboli began about 200,000 years ago. Through countless eruptions, lava built up around cracks in the Mediterranean seafloor. Eventually the buildup of lava reached sea level and started forming the volcanic island.

eXpert Tip

ACCORDING TO THE INTERNATIONAL ASSOCIATION OF VOLCANOLOGY AND CHEMISTRY OF THE EARTH'S INTERIOR, scientists and anyone else visiting an active volcano should first learn what happens right before that volcano erupts—so they can be on the lookout for things like shock waves. They should also "always be alert and avoid hasty action." We didn't follow those tips on Stromboli, and it could have cost us our lives. Bolting the way we did was foolish. With our backs toward the crater, we wouldn't be able to see if a lava bomb was coming at us. That's an important lesson. You may never have to dodge flying blobs of lava, but when faced with a dangerous situation, understand what the dangers are. Then you can take careful actions to avoid them.

MOUNT STROMBOLI
IS ONE OF ABOUT
60 VOLCANOES ON LAND THAT ERUPT AT LEAST
ONCE A YEAR.

Some volcanoes, like Stromboli, erupt frequently. Stromboli's eruptions are mild, with lava spitting into the air every 20 minutes or so. It looks a bit like soup on a high boil spattering out of the pot. Other volcanoes erupt violently, launching a tremendous amount of ash and gases high into the atmosphere. Mild eruptions build up mountains. Violent eruptions blow them apart.

What actually causes an eruption? The answer lies deep beneath the volcano. There, usually 1 to 6 miles (1.6 to 10 km) down, magma collects in a huge pocket called a magma chamber. It is this magma that fuels the volcano. How? It's all about pressure—and lots of gas.

Magma is more than melted rock. This hot slushy mixture also contains a lot of dissolved gases. Pressure from the overlying rocks holds the gases in the magma. But what happens when that pressure is relieved? Well, it's like opening a can of soda. The main ingredient in any soda is carbonated water, which is water with carbon dioxide gas dissolved in it. The can is sealed under pressure so that the carbon dioxide stays in the watery mixture. When you pop the tab, you relieve the pressure. That allows the gas to expand and form all those fizzy bubbles that rise to the top. If you shake the can right before opening it, you create more and bigger bubbles and the pressure increases. Open the can and . . . *PSSHHHH!* Bubbles and soda burst out all over.

The same sort of thing happens with the gases in magma. Cracks in Earth's surface, like vents, relieve the pressure on the magma. The dissolved gases expand, which means the gas molecules zip and zoom faster and farther apart, forming bubbles within the magma. The gas bubbles are lighter than the liquid magma, so they rise. The force of the expanding gas and rising bubbles pushes the magma up through the volcano. Higher and higher the bubbly brew rises until the volcano erupts. If the vent is plugged with rock, the pressure in the magma can build. When the pressure becomes too much . . . BOOM! A violent eruption blasts from the volcano, like a giant exploding can of soda.

A BLAST FROM BELOW

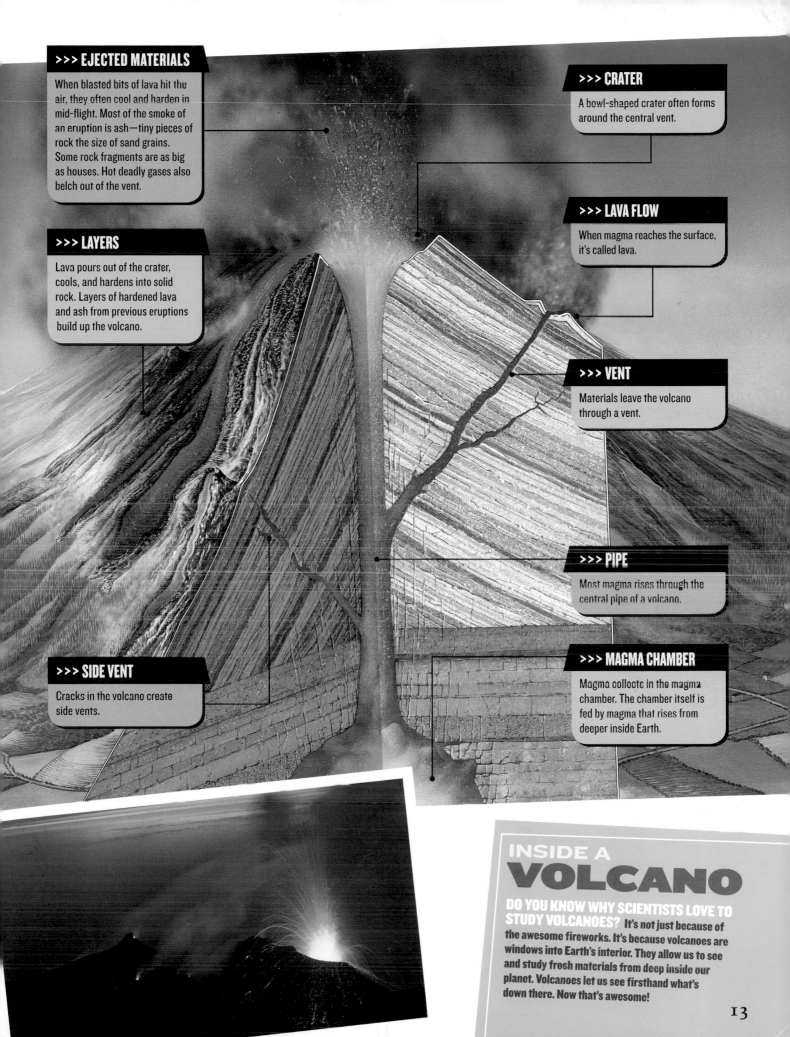

>>> EJECTED MATERIALS

When blasted bits of lava hit the air, they often cool and harden in mid-flight. Most of the smoke of an eruption is ash—tiny pieces of rock the size of sand grains. Some rock fragments are as big as houses. Hot deadly gases also belch out of the vent.

>>> LAYERS

Lava pours out of the crater, cools, and hardens into solid rock. Layers of hardened lava and ash from previous eruptions build up the volcano.

>>> SIDE VENT

Cracks in the volcano create side vents.

>>> CRATER

A bowl-shaped crater often forms around the central vent.

>>> LAVA FLOW

When magma reaches the surface, it's called lava.

>>> VENT

Materials leave the volcano through a vent.

>>> PIPE

Most magma rises through the central pipe of a volcano.

>>> MAGMA CHAMBER

Magma collects in the magma chamber. The chamber itself is fed by magma that rises from deeper inside Earth.

INSIDE A
VOLCANO

DO YOU KNOW WHY SCIENTISTS LOVE TO STUDY VOLCANOES? It's not just because of the awesome fireworks. It's because volcanoes are windows into Earth's interior. They allow us to see and study fresh materials from deep inside our planet. Volcanoes let us see firsthand what's down there. Now that's awesome!

13

INTO THE PIT

CARSTEN DESCENDS TO THE LAVA LAKE OF MOUNT NYIRAGONGO

A scientist, at top, lowers himself from the crater rim to the second terrace. Above, an expedition member walks on the hardened lava of Nyiragongo's crater floor.

Inside the crater atop Mount Nyiragongo lies the world's largest lava lake.

Gear & Gadgets

WE SOMETIMES USE a thermal suit when working close to lava. It's not exactly made for comfort—you can't bend easily, your vision is limited, and you're drenched in sweat. It does protect you from much of the lava's heat. But even in a special suit, you aren't protected enough to survive a direct hit from a lava bomb.

Notes From the Field

HOW DO YOU HAUL A WEEK'S WORTH OF WATER, FOOD, GEAR, AND EQUIPMENT UP AN 11,000-FOOT-TALL (3,353 m) MOUNTAIN? With the help of more than 100 porters! They are the unsung heroes of every expedition. We usually have no trouble finding enough local people to help carry our supplies. While the work is hard, our porters at Nyiragongo earned a month's salary in one day.

FROM THE RIM, THE CRATER LOOKED LIKE A GIANT BULL'S-EYE.

Two wide ledges, or terraces, ringed the inside of the crater. The third terrace formed the crater's flat floor. In the middle of that floor, as if in a giant soup bowl, a lake of lava bubbled and spat. That was our destination.

We had trudged nearly two miles up to the top of Mount Nyiragongo—a volcano in the African nation of the Democratic Republic of the Congo. Now my assistant and I were about to climb a quarter mile (400 m) down into the crater. No doubt it was dangerous. In fact, the scientists on the expedition were concerned that the lava lake—the world's largest—would overflow its bowl-shaped spatter cone and flood the crater floor. After some discussion, and knowing the risk, we prepared to descend into the mouth of one of Earth's most active volcanoes.

The rope strained as we lowered ourselves down the steep crater walls, kicking aside loose rocks along the way. The glowing lava illuminated those walls, which soon loomed above us. I suddenly felt very small.

Finally we reached the crater floor of hardened lava. Talk about feeling small. The roar of the bubbly cauldron was deafening. Nasty smelling, lethal gases swirled around us. I could feel the warmth through my shoes as we approached the fiery lake.

Standing next to the lava lake, we actually couldn't see the lava. It was hidden from our view by the 40-foot-tall (12 m) spatter cone. That's the wall of solid rock that forms around the edge of the lake as the spattering lava cools and hardens. It's like being an ant on a table next to a bowl of hot tomato soup. The ant would have to climb up the outside of the bowl to see the soup. Well, this ant (me!) wanted to see that bubbling soup. Besides, I needed to get a sample of freshly hardened lava for the scientists to study. The only way to do that was to climb the wall and grab a hot chunk from the rim.

High above us, the scientists watched the lava lake carefully through binoculars. They could radio us if they saw violent bubbling or rising lava near our side of the lake. All was clear, so up I went. The quick climb up the crumbly rock and ash was like running on marbles. Suddenly I reached the top. I peeked into the bubbling lake.

The experience was mind-blowing. Lava splattered into all kinds of shapes, stretching and snapping apart in midair. The heat was nearly unbearable. The most amazing thing, though, was that I could actually feel the volcano. It was like standing on a gigantic loudspeaker with the bass turned up. With each burst of gas, booming shock waves rumbled through my body.

Quickly, I grabbed a hunk of fresh hot rock. Even with my special heat-resistant gloves, I could barely hold it. I jumped and slid down the wall back to the crater floor, my heart pounding from another extreme adventure.

Waves of lava lap over the rim of Nyiragongo's spatter cone.

VOLCANIC FORCES

A CRACKED-UP PLANET

WHEN YOU WITNESS THE AWESOME POWER OF NYIRAGONGO,

one question comes to mind: What incredible force created this? You already know part of the answer. Magma from a chamber beneath the mountain feeds the lava lake and fuels eruptions. But there's more to the story.

Earth's crust—the rocky skin that covers the planet—is broken into about 20 slabs called tectonic plates. Many of the plates are huge. The Pacific plate alone includes most of the Pacific Ocean floor. The North American plate consists of almost all of North America and Greenland plus half of the North Atlantic floor.

Wherever two plates meet, you find Earth at its most extreme. That's because plates move. It's a slow go. On average, plates creep just a few centimeters a year—about as fast as your fingernails grow. But that slow motion really packs a wallop. Where plates slide past each other, sections might snag for years before breaking loose suddenly and releasing pent-up energy as trembling earthquakes.

Where plates collide, one plate often dives beneath the other. The leading edge of the sinking plate melts in Earth's hot interior. The magma rises, collects in chambers, and may eventually punch through the surface as volcanoes.

Where plates move apart, the crust stretches and cracks. Magma rises through the openings. This kind of plate motion happens mostly on the ocean floor, hidden from view. But in a few places, we get to witness it on land. And guess what? The region around Nyiragongo is one of those places.

One of the local Maasai people looks out over the Great Rift Valley, formed by one of Earth's tectonic plates splitting apart.

>>> PAST

Forces deep in the Earth began pulling the African plate apart. At the same time, magma pushed up from below. Cracks formed and filled with magma. Volcanoes formed.

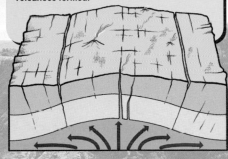

>>> PRESENT

As the crust stretches and cracks, huge blocks of rock drop. They become the walls of a long, wide, and deep rift valley. Volcanic activity continues.

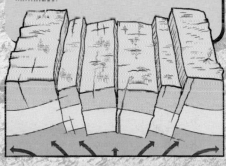

>>> FUTURE

As the land continues to rip apart, or rift, one plate may become two. Over millions of years, the rift valley may deepen and lengthen enough to reach the ocean and flood. That flooded land will be the beginning of an ever widening sea, creating a new ocean between what could be two new continents.

TECTONIC PLATES

Earthquakes and volcanoes clearly mark plate boundaries.

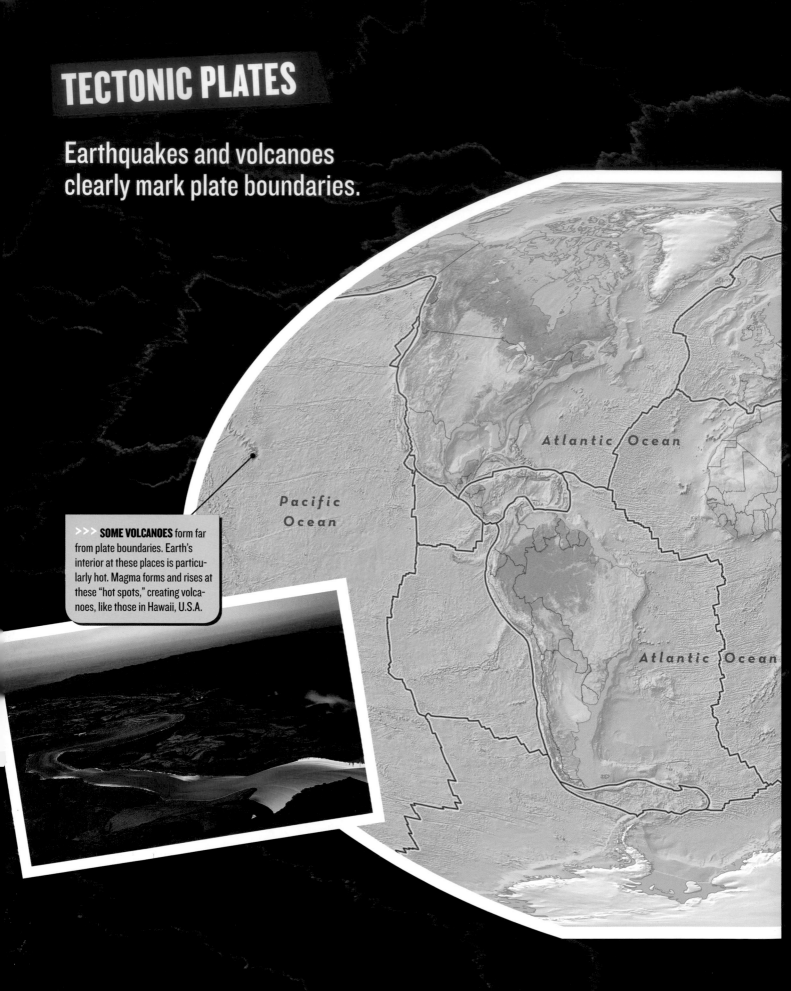

>>> **SOME VOLCANOES** form far from plate boundaries. Earth's interior at these places is particularly hot. Magma forms and rises at these "hot spots," creating volcanoes, like those in Hawaii, U.S.A.

Atlantic Ocean

Pacific Ocean

Atlantic Ocean

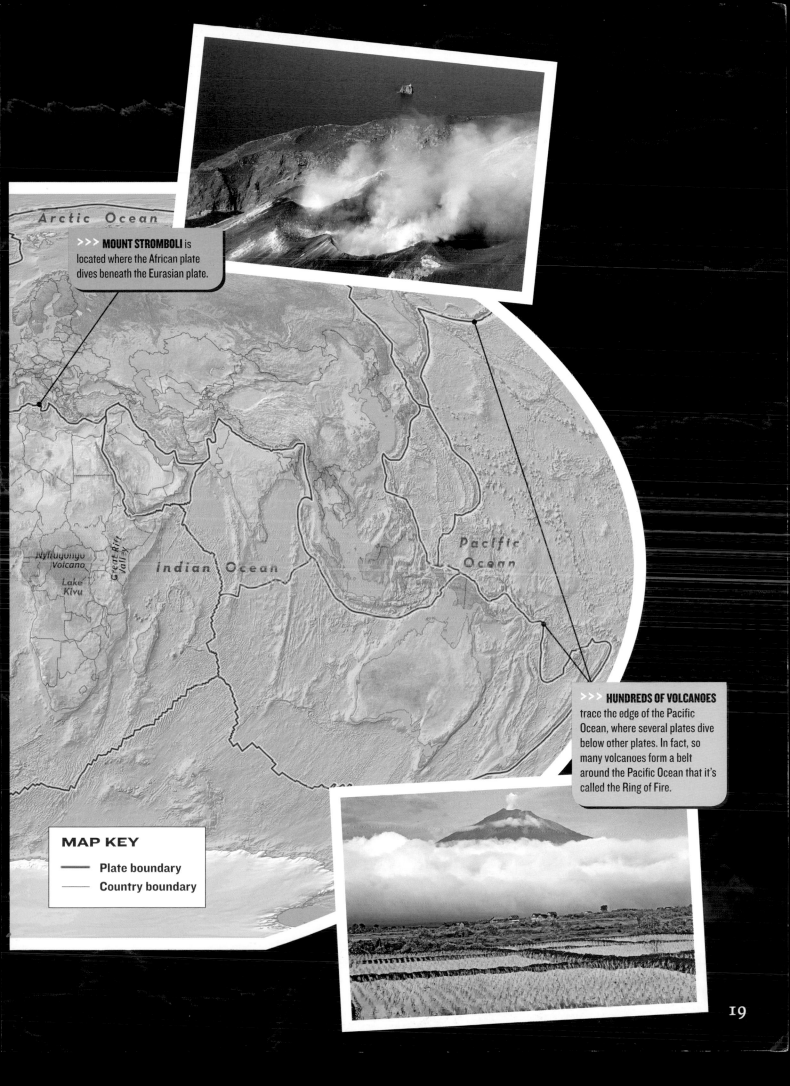

Arctic Ocean

>>> **MOUNT STROMBOLI** is located where the African plate dives beneath the Eurasian plate.

Nyiragongo Volcano

Great Rift Valley

Lake Kivu

Indian Ocean

Pacific Ocean

>>> **HUNDREDS OF VOLCANOES** trace the edge of the Pacific Ocean, where several plates dive below other plates. In fact, so many volcanoes form a belt around the Pacific Ocean that it's called the Ring of Fire.

MAP KEY

—— Plate boundary

—— Country boundary

CARSTEN'S ADVENTURE—
ON THE MORNING OF
JANUARY 17, 2002,

the rift valley around Mount Nyiragongo spread apart just a little bit more. It wasn't much, but it was sudden. The jolt opened up cracks, or fissures, on the sides of the mountain, some a couple miles long. Lava gushed and oozed from the fissures. The lava lake drained and liquid lava raced down the slopes, possibly as fast as 60 miles an hour (100 km/h). Huge rivers of lava destroyed everything in their path. One of those fiery rivers headed straight toward the nearby city of Goma—and its 400,000 inhabitants.

Within hours, the lava was creeping through the heart of the city, like a hot-tempered bulldozer. Another large fissure opened near the airport, with lava blanketing much of the runway. Smaller cracks split open all over town. Farther away, the slower moving lava gave residents time to flee, but still, more than one hundred people died. Many of the deaths resulted from collapsed buildings and the volcano's lethal gases.

By day's end, much of the city lay in ruins. Burned-out cars and scorched buildings were engulfed in several feet of lava, which was now cooling into solid black rock. The smell of sulfur lingered in the air. Billowy clouds of steam and sharp hisses arose from the shore of Lake Kivu as the lava made its way into the water and quickly cooled.

All told, the lava flows had destroyed 4,500 homes, leaving nearly 100,000 people homeless. But within days, the courageous people of Goma returned to the city, determined to rebuild their homes and their lives.

The heat from lava flows set much of Goma ablaze.

People cross over hardened lava to return to Goma just a few days after the 2002 eruption of Mount Nyiragongo devastated the city.

AFTERMATH OF AN ERUPTION

NATURE'S SIGNAL

THE VOLCANOLOGIST DIEUDONNE WAFULAH KNEW IT WAS COMING. He had been studying Nyiragongo for years and recognized the telltale signs of an eruption: The lava in the lava lake had been getting higher for weeks. Minor to moderate earthquakes had been increasing, too, along with the release of gas from the crater. These were all signs that magma was rising underground and ready to burst out. Wafulah warned the government and as many people as he could before the volcano erupted.

Residents of Goma built new houses on the hardened lava of the 2002 eruption.

EXTREME LIVING

MOUNT NYIRAGONGO ERUPTED ON A THURSDAY

and by then nearly everyone had evacuated safely. On Monday, thousands of people were making their way back into the city. The top several feet of lava had cooled enough to form a rocky crust. Returning residents tested the crust gingerly, then walked across it, even as the river of liquid lava continued to flow underneath.

You might wonder how people could live in such extreme conditions. Why would they stay in the shadow of an active volcano? For most, there is little choice. Many people in the region are poor and cannot afford to move far away. Besides, Nyiragongo provides important resources. Lava rock from past eruptions breaks down into rich soil that supports forests and crops. In addition, Lake Kivu provides one of the most important resources of all—water.

So, the people of Goma rebuilt on top of the old lava flow. They have learned to live with the risk of the future eruptions that are sure to come.

People of Goma often use handmade wooden bikes to haul resources down the mountain.

LAKE KIVU IS NO ORDINARY LAKE. IT EXPLODES!

LARGE AMOUNTS OF CARBON DIOXIDE AND METHANE GAS ARE DISSOLVED IN THE WATER AT THE BOTTOM OF THE LAKE. ON RARE OCCASIONS, THIS GAS RISES VIOLENTLY AND EXPLODES FROM THE WATER. IF THIS HAPPENED OVER LARGE AREAS OF THE LAKE, THE AMOUNT OF GAS COULD KILL THOUSANDS OF PEOPLE. EARTHQUAKES AND VOLCANIC ERUPTIONS COULD TRIGGER SUCH EXPLOSIONS. FORTUNATELY THIS DID NOT HAPPEN DURING THE 2002 ERUPTION.

HOW TO COMPARE LAVAS

HOW FAST CAN LAVA FLOW? Some lava is so thick that you could walk faster than the lava flows. For other lava flows, you'd need a bike to outpace it. The thinnest, runniest lava can flow at 60 miles an hour (100 km/h)—as fast as a car on the highway! That's how fast lava traveled at Nyiragongo during a 1977 eruption. It was much slower in 2002.

Let's use some liquids you might find in your kitchen to understand the thicknesses of different kinds of lava. TRY THIS: >>>

BE EARTH FRIENDLY

THE DEADLY METHANE AT THE BOTTOM OF Lake Kivu can be put to good use. Projects are under way to try and pump out the methane–carbon dioxide gas mixture. The methane is separated and burned to generate electricity. It's a lot cleaner than burning coal, oil, or even wood. The carbon dioxide is then pumped back into the lake. Because the process is complex, it's still being tested, but without the methane, the chance of deadly lake explosions may be reduced. Using clean energy and making the lake safer—how Earth friendly is that!

Fishing / Lake Kivu

>>> PENNY DROP

1. Half-fill three clear plastic cups with one of each of these liquids: corn syrup, cooking oil, and water.

2. Drop a penny in each of the cups and use a stopwatch or clock with a second hand to time how long the penny takes to hit the bottom of the cup.

3. Which liquid do you think represents the thickest lava? Which represents the thinnest?

4. This table shows different types of lavas arranged by how easily they flow. Which liquid do you think corresponds to each type of lava?

FELSIC LAVA	ANDESITIC LAVA	MAFIC LAVA
Coolest lava; flows most slowly	Hotter lava; flows more quickly	Hottest lava; flows fastest

>>> LAVA RACE

1. Prop up one end of a cookie sheet on a few books to make a ramp. Place a few paper towels at the bottom of the sheet.

2. With two friends, prepare to pour a teaspoonful of each of the liquids near the top of the ramp. Predict the order in which you think the liquids will reach the bottom of the ramp. Be sure to pour at the same time and the same height on the ramp. Start the race!

3. Compare the results of the race with your prediction.

25

A glacier in Iceland breaks apart near the ocean in the warmer climate.

CHAPTER 2

>>> Glaciers
& Ice Sheets

[Glaciers—Large masses of ice that slowly move downhill; Ice sheets—Huge masses of ice that cover a wide area of land]

JOURNEY INTO A GLACIER

THE ICY WALLS THAT SURROUNDED ME SPARKLED A BRILLIANT BLUE.

These icy lumps are called "ice balls." They build up as wind blows a spray of tiny water droplets into the shaft. In the summertime, huge waterfalls plunge into the shaft. But because it was autumn, only spray remained, freezing as it hit the surface and accumulating in icy knobs and chunks—the ice balls!

I had never seen such an incredible color. It was like being in the middle of a giant glittering sapphire. Looking up, I squinted against the blinding sunshine that beamed through the distant opening.

It was a beautiful scene, but danger was all around. We were inside a deep shaft in the middle of a glacier that covers most of Greenland. I clung to a rope that was anchored into the ice at the top of the shaft. The rest of the rope dangled to the bottom a few hundred feet below. If my climbing equipment failed, I wouldn't survive the fall.

There were other dangers. Without warning, the weight of the glacier could squeeze out chunks of ice from the walls and blast them across the shaft. I didn't want to be in the way.

Ice from above wasn't safe, either. Climbers accidentally knock off icy bits with their ice axes or their spiked boots, called crampons. These falling shards of ice become dangerous missiles to anyone below. That's one reason we wear helmets.

As I slid a few more feet into the depths of the glacier, I focused on a trickle of water dripping down the wall. The September air, though brisk, was warm enough to melt a small amount of ice during the day. My eyes followed the trickle of meltwater all the way to the bottom of the shaft. There it dripped into a pool. Soon I was hovering over that pool. Then, suddenly, I was in it!

While I had planned a little swim, the moment of impact was still shocking, and shockingly cold! I'm glad I wore a dry suit. This type of scuba diving suit seals at the neck and wrists to keep the body dry. It kept me warm enough to swim in water that was close to or even just a bit below freezing. Still, I could take the cold water for only thirty minutes. My great Arctic swim had come to an end. So it was back to the rope for a grueling—and sweaty—return climb to the top.

The shaft that we explored in Greenland is a type of glacier cave. Glaciers can be thousands of feet thick. But they are not smooth, continuous masses of ice throughout. Instead they are riddled with deep shafts, twisting passageways, and other openings. What carves out these icy caves?

Inside a glacial cave,
upper Aletsch glacier,
Switzerland

Water and heat are the main sculptors. During the short summers, the warmth melts some ice on the surface, creating streams of meltwater. These streams rush into cracks and potholes in the ice. The swirling torrents of water widen the cracks and deepen the potholes. Year after year, this force of moving water eventually creates caves that sometimes reach all the way to the bottom of the glacier.

Unlike rock caves that barely change over a century, glacier caves change with the seasons. Each summer, when temperatures rise, a rush of water noticeably shapes and reshapes glacier caves. You can see this type of force if you hold an ice cube under a running faucet. The force and warmth of the water—warmer than the ice, anyway—quickly dissolves the cube.

Notes from the Field

GLACIER CAVES HAVE A WAY OF SNEAKING UP ON YOU. During an expedition in Iceland, I was walking on the surface of a glacier when suddenly I crashed through thin ice into a cave with a river running through it. I lost my cameras in the swift current, but friends were able to pull me to safety. This close call was a reminder to never explore extreme places alone.

Speaking of warmth, sometimes heat alone is enough to carve out caves. If a volcano is nearby, heat might escape through vents and melt out hollows of ice along the bottom of the glacier. This happens a lot in Iceland. That island country straddles a rift valley on the Atlantic Ocean floor where two plates are splitting apart. The volcanic activity from between the plates provides heat that creates some spectacular glacier caves.

>>> SUMMER

Glacier caves change drastically with the seasons. Summer temperatures in parts of Greenland can reach 50ºF (10ºC). The resulting meltwater plunges into the ice shafts as raging waterfalls. The crashing force of the water reshapes the ice throughout the season.

>>> AUTUMN

As temperatures drop, water freezes and stops pouring into the caves. This is the prime season for exploring glacier caves.

>>> WINTER

The strong winds and deep cold of winter often freeze cave entrances shut. Without flowing water, new caves don't form. But many caves collapse as the glacier itself continues to creep a few inches toward the ocean. And there is the threat of avalanches!

POLAR ENVIRONMENTS

This ice on Mount Erebus has been shaped by the wind. Ross Island, Antarctica.

MY EXPLORATIONS HAVE TAKEN ME ALL AROUND THE WORLD.

In many ways, no place is more extreme than the regions near the top and bottom of our planet. In the north lie Greenland, Iceland, and other places within or near the Arctic Circle. In the south, the continent of Antarctica lies almost entirely within the Antarctic Circle.

As you might guess, both of these regions are cold, icy worlds. An ice sheet 1 to 2 miles (1.6–3.2 km) thick covers most of Greenland. An even larger blanket of ice covers nearly all of Antarctica. Each ice sheet built up over many thousands of years. The weight of countless snowfalls compressed earlier buried snow into layers of ice. The ice pushes outward from its thickest region. It's like cake batter spreading outward as you pour it in a pan—but a lot slower!

The ice creeps under its own weight toward the sea. Near the coast, the ice sheet often divides into individual glaciers that fill coastal valleys. At the water's edge, chunks of ice break off into the sea. These icebergs float away until they melt in warmer waters.

Here are some other cool facts about these cold places. Which ones surprise you most?

NATURE'S SIGNAL

IN SOUTHERN GREENLAND, ARCTIC HARES ARE BROWN IN SUMMER. It's a good color for blending in with the rocks, soil, and plants. But during the long winter, brown hares would be easy to spot by predators such as wolves and foxes. Over thousands of years, arctic hares adapted for protection, turning white in autumn. They still have to keep a watchful eye though: Arctic foxes also turn white in autumn. In fact, several animals do. Changing fur or feather color is one of nature's signals that seasons are changing.

GREENLAND		ANTARCTICA
Average winter temperatures: 21°F (-6.1°C) in the south and minus 31°F (-35°C) in the north; average summer temperatures: 45°F (7.2°C) in the south and 39°F (3.9°C) in the north; precipitation: 24 inches (61 cm) per year in the south and 2 inches (5 cm) in the north	**CLIMATE**	Average winter temperature at McMurdo Station (a research center on an island off the coast): minus 15°F (-26.1°C); average summer temperature: 27°F (-2.8°C); precipitation: 8 inches (20 cm) per year
A variety of colorful plants cover the ice-free valleys near the coast during the short summers. Most plants grow low to the ground, like crowberry shrubs and the national flower, the broad-leaved fireweed.	**PLANTS**	Only two kinds of plants with stems and roots are native to Antarctica. One is called hair grass. The other is called pearlwort. The only other plants that grow here are mosses.
Land animals include arctic foxes, arctic wolves, reindeer, and polar bears. A variety of seals and whales swim near shore. Snowy owls, gulls, and many other birds take to the skies.	**ANIMALS**	This is home to whales and penguins. While penguins don't fly, they are long-distance walkers and excellent swimmers. Other birds include albatrosses and petrels.
About 57,000 people live in Greenland, along the coast. Most work in the fishing industry.	**PEOPLE**	There are no permanent residents in Antarctica. Between 1,000 and 5,000 scientists and staff live at research stations for months at a time.

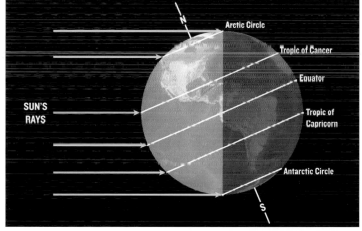

During summer in the Northern Hemisphere, the North Pole points toward the sun. At this time of year, at least some locations within the Arctic Circle are always in sunshine. There is no dark night. This endless daylight lasts for six months near the pole, but for only a few weeks at the Arctic Circle. At this same time, at least some locations within the Antarctic Circle are always in darkness. The situation reverses six months later, when the South Pole is in endless daylight and the North Pole is in endless darkness.

Looks like a nice afternoon on a winter's day, right? Wrong. It's midnight in the summer! Welcome to the land of the midnight sun!

33

PACIFIC
OCEAN
180°

Alaska
(U.S.)

Chukchi
Sea

East Siberian
Sea

150°W

75°N

150°E

Beaufort
Sea

Limit of
summer ice

New Siberian
Islands

Laptev
Sea

Banks
Island

Victoria
Island

ARCTIC

CANADA

RUSSIA

90°W

North
Pole

Kara
Sea

Ellesmere
Island

OCEAN

Franz Josef
Land

Baffin
Island

Baffin
Bay

60°W

Greenland
(Denmark)

Novaya
Zemlya

60°E

Svalbard
(Norway)

Barents
Sea

30°E

Greenland Sea

ICELAND

ARCTIC CIRCLE

Norwegian Sea

NORWAY

SWEDEN

FINLAND

30°W

ATLANTIC
OCEAN

0°

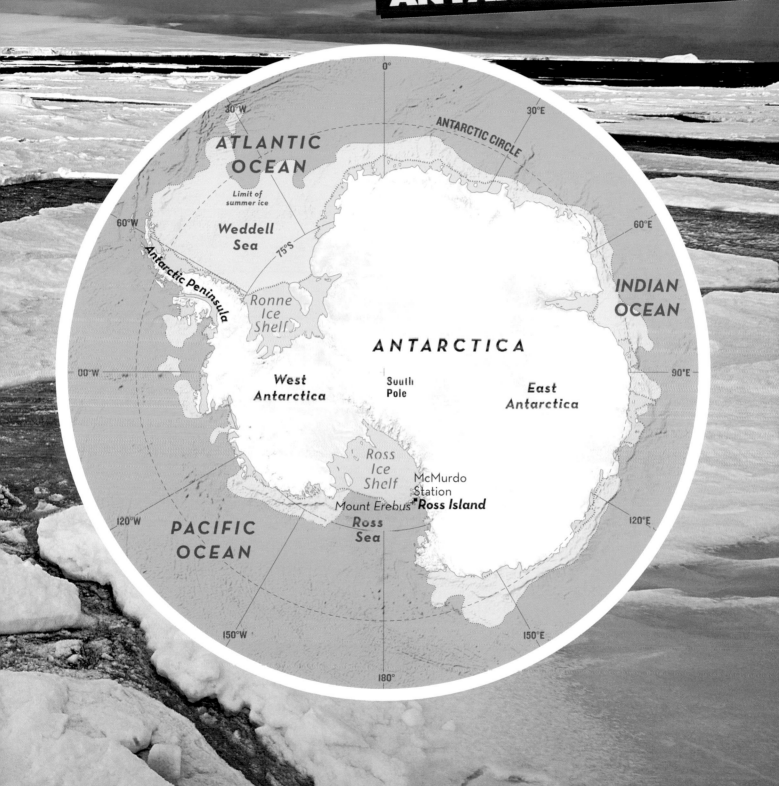

ATLANTIC
OCEAN

*Limit of
summer ice*

**Weddell
Sea**

ANTARCTIC CIRCLE

INDIAN
OCEAN

Antarctic Peninsula

*Ronne
Ice
Shelf*

**West
Antarctica**

ANTARCTICA

South
Pole

**East
Antarctica**

*Ross
Ice
Shelf*

McMurdo
Station

Mount Erebus **Ross Island**

**Ross
Sea**

PACIFIC
OCEAN

0°

30°W

30°E

60°W

60°E

75°S

90°W

90°E

120°W

120°E

150°W

150°E

180°

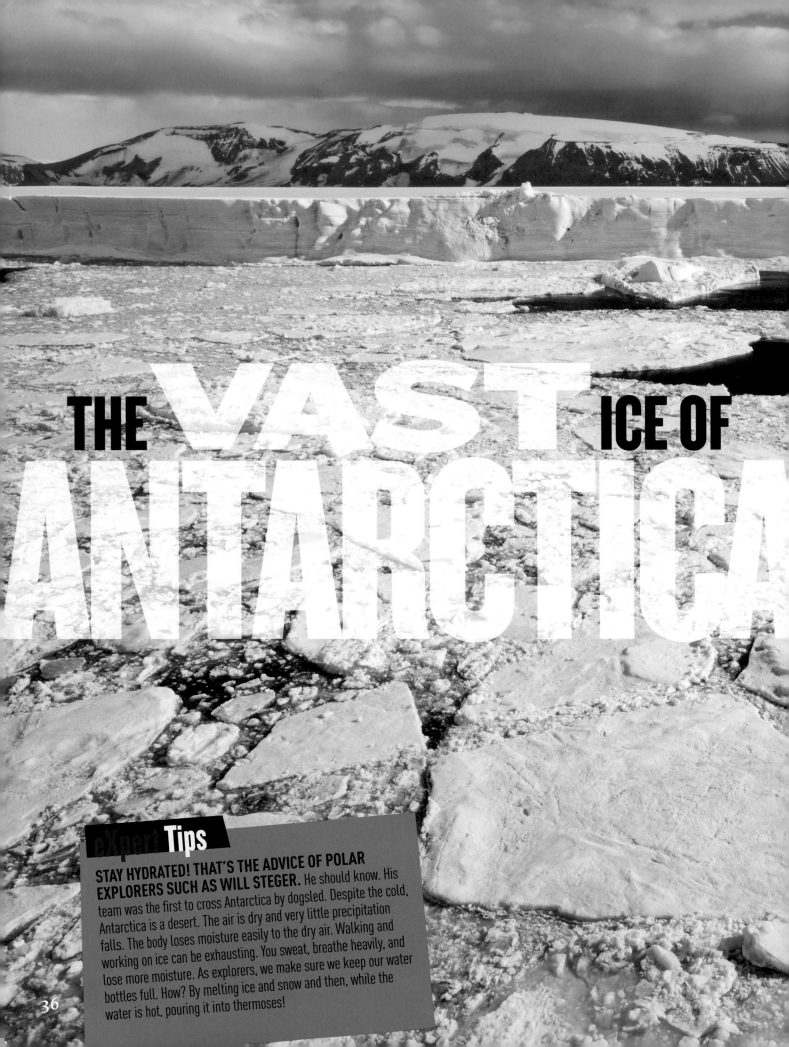

THE VAST ICE OF ANTARCTICA

eXpert Tips

STAY HYDRATED! THAT'S THE ADVICE OF POLAR EXPLORERS SUCH AS WILL STEGER. He should know. His team was the first to cross Antarctica by dogsled. Despite the cold, Antarctica is a desert. The air is dry and very little precipitation falls. The body loses moisture easily to the dry air. Walking and working on ice can be exhausting. You sweat, breathe heavily, and lose more moisture. As explorers, we make sure we keep our water bottles full. How? By melting ice and snow and then, while the water is hot, pouring it into thermoses!

HERE'S THE THING ABOUT ANTARCTICA— IT'S BIG.

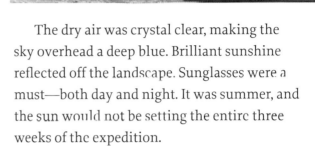

No, not just big—vast! Dictionaries define *vast* as immense, empty, and boundless. All of these words describe Antarctica. But so do these words— fantastic, awesome, otherworldly, and beautiful.

When I first stepped from the plane onto the Antarctic ice, I knew I was in a place like no other. I was struck by the sameness of my surroundings. A nearly flat plain of ice stretched to the horizon in most directions. We were on an island, but you'd never know it. Thick sea ice connected the island to the mainland about 45 miles (72 km) away.

The dry air was crystal clear, making the sky overhead a deep blue. Brilliant sunshine reflected off the landscape. Sunglasses were a must—both day and night. It was summer, and the sun would not be setting the entire three weeks of the expedition.

The constant sunshine did little to warm the air. Temperatures mostly stayed in the negative numbers. Lows were down to minus 30°F (34°C). Strange things happen when it gets that cold. The slightest amount of moisture glazes ropes with ice. That makes them tricky to hold. Eating is a challenge, too. My parents used to say, "Eat your food before it gets cold." Here we say, "Eat your food before it freezes." You might end up chiseling frozen soup from a bowl that was hot from the stove a few minutes earlier.

The vastness of Antarctica really makes you feel exposed to the weather, especially when the wind blows. I often had to turn away from the stinging ice crystals that the wind whipped at us. During some days (or were they nights?), the tents rattled and flapped so much I thought for sure they were going to fly away.

Everything about Antarctica was extreme and beautiful. But the sight I'll remember most occurred several days into the expedition. We took a short helicopter ride from our base camp. We landed about halfway up a mountain. I stepped off. I looked up. I don't know how long I gawked at the steaming volcano, Mount Erebus, that loomed before me.

Gear & Gadgets

WHEN IT COMES TO STAYING WARM, the point isn't to keep cold air out. It's to keep your body heat in. Sometimes when sleeping on the tent floor, the heat from my body melted the ice beneath my sleeping bag. To keep my body heat from escaping, I dress in layers. I sleep in layers, too. In Antarctica, my "bed" consisted of a fleece liner inside a sleeping bag stuffed inside another sleeping bag. I laid the double bags on top of a sheepskin rug on top of an air mattress on top of a foam mat. It took six layers of bedding and as many layers of clothing to keep me warm.

LAND OF FIRE AND ICE

I WAS LOOKING AT MOUNT EREBUS. IT'S THE SOUTHERN-MOST ACTIVE VOLCANO IN THE WORLD. IT'S ALSO A MOUNTAIN OF EXTREMES.

Temperatures on the crater rim can dip to minus 40°F (-40°C) in summer. Yet inside the crater, a fiery lava lake boils. The lake shoots out lava bombs into the chilly air during mild eruptions. How did this mountain of fire and ice form at the bottom of the world?

It turns out that a series of rift valleys lies deep beneath the Antarctic ice sheet. These valleys result from the Antarctic plate slowly stretching apart. The stretching cracks the crust. Magma breaks through and forms volcanoes.

The heat of Erebus melts out a maze of icy caves. The heat shapes the surface, too. Vents on the side of the mountain release a steamy mix of gases, mostly water vapor. The moisture freezes in the cold air. Crystal by crystal, ice towers build up around the vent. Some reach 60 feet (18 m) tall. Winds sculpt the towers into fantastic shapes. It's an unbelievable site.

MOUNT EREBUS IS A WELL-STUDIED VOLCANO. SCIENTISTS EVEN HAVE A WEBCAM ON THE RIM OF THE CRATER.

LIFE UNDER A MICROSCOPE

YOU DON'T SEE MUCH LIFE ON MOUNT EREBUS—unless you have a microscope. In certain places, the volcano's heat melts the ice and forms patches of hot soil. These patches are full of microscopic life, or microbes, like bacteria.

It may seem impossible for tiny life-forms to survive in the harsh Antarctic without fur or insulation. But not only do they survive—they thrive. In fact, these microbes are called extremophiles because they love the extreme conditions that would kill most other organisms. Extremophiles live in other unusual places, too, like the vents of poisonous gases on the ocean floor. They also form the rainbow colors of scalding acid pools in Yellowstone National Park.

Some extremophiles even survive in outer space. In the 1970s, astronauts brought back from the moon a camera from a spacecraft that had landed there a couple years earlier. Foam padding around the camera contained bacteria. The microbes must have gotten inside when the camera was built. After the trip back to Earth, the bacteria were still alive! They had survived years of no air, extreme temperatures, and radiation from the sun.

Antarctica has its share of extremophiles. And scientists want to know more about them. What kinds of microbes are they? Where did they come from? Did they blow in on the winds? Did Erebus spit them out during eruptions? Did some come from outer space? Studies have shown that when large meteorites collide with planets, the impact blasts surface rocks into space. What if these rocks contained microbes that made it to Earth? Scientists are trying to answer these and other questions about Antarctica's most extreme life-forms.

Extremophile

Acid pool / Yellowstone National Park

A CHANGING POLAR WORLD

THE POLAR LANDSCAPE IS CHANGING, AND NOT JUST FROM ICE CAVES AND ICE TOWERS.

Polar ice is melting faster than it has in the past. Ice sheets and glaciers always melt a bit in the summer. But the winter snows and cold temperatures usually replenish what melts. In recent years, this balance has been thrown out of whack. Now, more ice melts in summer than forms in winter.

Most of this meltwater finds its way into the ocean. You know what that means—a rise in sea level. Over the past 20 years, sea level has risen more than one-tenth of an inch (2.5 cm) per year. That may not seem like much, but the effects of even small increases are huge. Storm waves become more destructive. Flooding increases. Animals lose more of their habitat.

So why is ice melting faster than usual? What's going on? The answer is global warming.

Since 1880, the average global temperature has risen approximately 1.4°F (0.8°C). The increase is at least twice as much in most of the polar world. The reason is the melting ice. In many places, the sun shines on dark water or land where it used to shine on white ice. Light colors reflect sunlight; dark colors absorb it. So with less ice, polar regions are warming up faster than places that had no ice to begin with.

The recent surge in temperatures is due largely to human activities. When people burn fossil fuels, like coal and oil, carbon dioxide and other gases pour into the air. These gases trap more of the sun's heat and make our planet warmer. Plants use carbon dioxide. But when we cut down trees, there are fewer plants to take the carbon dioxide out of the air.

In 2007 a route through the part of the Arctic Ocean known as the Northwest Passage became ice free for the first time in recorded history.

RUSSIA

ARCTIC OCEAN

ICELAND

75°N

Limit of summer ice

150°W

Greenland (Denmark)

ARCTIC CIRCLE

Alaska (U.S.)

Beaufort Sea

Banks Island

Baffin Bay

Victoria Island

Baffin Island

Limit of winter ice

60°N

60°W

Hudson Bay

90°W

CANADA

MAP KEY

—— Northwest Passage

BE EARTH FRIENDLY

WHAT CAN YOU DO TO REDUCE GLOBAL WARMING? Plenty!
Whenever you use fewer fossil fuels and resources, you help. Start with these tips:

- Turn off lights, TVs, and computers when not in use.
- Walk or ride a bike instead of riding in a vehicle, when you can.
- Recycle materials as much as possible. Compost food and yard waste to use in a garden.
- Use energy-efficient light bulbs and appliances.
- Save water by not letting the faucet run when brushing your teeth. Water lawns and plants only as much as needed.
- Spread the word and keep informed. Tell your family and friends about these tips. Find out other ways to reduce global warming and fight pollution at the same time!

41

You can thank sunlight for the dazzling blue color of glacial ice. Sunlight is a combination of many colors, each traveling in waves of slightly different lengths. Combined, the different colors look white. But when sunlight passes through thick ice, the blue wavelengths are just the right size to break away from the rest of the colors and scatter throughout the ice. So the ice looks blue.

HOW TO TEST FABRICS FOR WARMTH

CLOTHES ARE MADE OF ALL SORTS OF FABRICS. Which ones would keep you warmest on a cold Arctic expedition? In other words, which fabrics hold in heat best? Let's do an experiment to find out.

>>> MATERIALS

> Five samples of different fabrics. You might try cotton, wool, denim, nylon, and fleece. All samples should be the same size, about 5 in. x 7 in. (12.7 x 17.8 cm), and about the same color (all dark colored or light colored).

> A pitcher of warm water

> Five clear plastic cups with lids (all same size and shape)

> Thermometer

> Masking tape

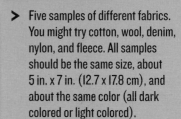

>>> STEPS

1. Predict which fabric you think will hold in heat the longest. Record your prediction.

2. Take the temperature of the water and record it.

3. Fill each cup with the same amount of water and close the lid.

4. Wrap each cup with a different fabric. Use masking tape to hold the fabric in place.

5. After 15 minutes, measure the temperature of each cup and record it.

6. Which fabric held in the heat of the water best? Which fabric let the most heat escape? How do your results compare to your prediction? Which fabric would be best for clothes on your expedition?

CHAPTER 3

>>> **Deserts**

[Places that receive less than ten inches (25.4 cm) of rainfall per year]

A Tuareg tribesman leads his camels through the dunes of the Sahara.

ACROSS THE SAHARA

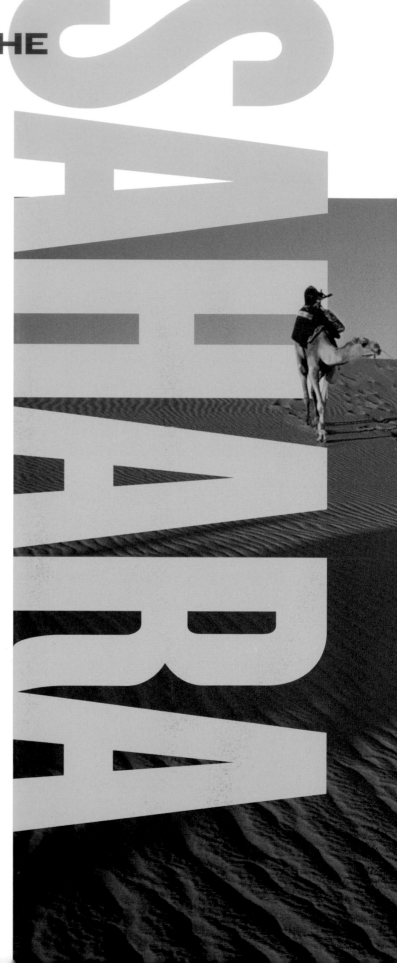

I LOVE TO EAT DATES.

I plucked a whole branch full and held them like a bouquet, popping one after another into my mouth. Suddenly, my traveling companion turned and stared at me, as if to say, "Hey, what about me?" I smiled. "Don't worry, I won't forget you." Instead of waiting for me to pass them to him, he leaned over. And with one enormous bite, he ate nearly half of the bouquet. Surprised, I broke into a chuckle. I had no idea a camel could be so impatient.

When I was a kid, I dreamed of all kinds of adventures. But I never imagined myself riding across the Sahara on a camel. Yet here I was swaying to and fro above the sand.

We were traveling from Lake Chad deep inside Africa all the way north to the coast of the Mediterranean Sea. The entire 100-day trip would cover 1,500 miles (2,414 km). The distance was like traveling from Texas north to the Canadian border. The experience, however, was unlike any trek through the United States. There are no grassy plains, no green forests, no streets, and often, not even trails.

Instead, we passed through some of the most brutal wilderness on Earth. Hard rocky ground with a few tufts of dried grass gave way to soft seas of sand with no vegetation at all. Spring-fed water holes surrounded by palm trees dotted our route. But these oases were few and far between.

46

The weather was just as fierce. Temperatures often soared above 100°F (37.8° C) during the day then plunged below freezing at night. The sun was intense. Shade was hard to come by. Winds, instead of bringing relief, blasted us with sand and small stones.

I was no stranger to these conditions. I had traveled across the Sahara several times on a motorcycle. But I was more excited to make the trip the ancient way—by camel. Our caravan consisted of 25 camels, some for riding and some for carrying supplies. For me, the camels were the real adventure. Each one had its own personality. Mine was especially moody. He could be cooperative and happy one day, then stubborn and grouchy the next. But we depended on each other and I like to think we became close friends.

Camels are built for the desert. They can survive a week or more without food or water. However, when they are working hard, they need to eat more often. So during one stretch of barren desert, we worried that we had not brought enough grass for the camels to eat. They were weak and tired. We feared some might die. We were heartbroken.

Then suddenly something appeared in the sand ahead. Grass! An earlier caravan had left extra grass scattered on the ground where they had camped overnight. We gathered every blade and fed the camels. The next day, we came upon another campsite with grass left behind. Our camels were saved!

There would be more tough days ahead. But our good fortune of finding food for the camels lifted our spirits as we continued our journey.

Below, Bedouin eat breakfast by campfire in the Acacus Mountains, Sahara, Libya.

Notes From the Field

WHAT DO YOU EAT ON A 100-DAY JOURNEY THROUGH THE SAHARA? Dates, dates, dates, and whatever the local guide cooks! Dinner was mostly pasta or rice with chili peppers and tomato sauce. Vegetables were added if we were able to buy them at an oasis. If we had meat, everything but the bones was mixed in with the pasta or rice. Leftovers were warmed up for breakfast. We also drank plenty of tea.

Different Types of DESERTS

HERE'S A TRICKY QUESTION YOU CAN ASK YOUR FRIENDS:
HOW ARE ANTARCTICA AND THE SAHARA ALIKE?

Let them guess before you give this answer: They both are deserts! You probably don't think of Antarctica as a desert, but like the Sahara, it receives less than ten inches (25.4 cm) of precipitation a year. That makes it a desert. Much of Greenland is a desert, too. Antarctica and Greenland are polar deserts.

There are many different kinds of deserts. Deserts along an ocean coast are coastal deserts. Imagine a sandy, rocky desert landscape complete with cacti alongside a blue sea. That's the Atacama, a coastal desert in Chile, South America. Pacific Ocean waves lap against its shores. Yet, the Atacama is the driest desert in the world! It averages about half an inch (1.3 cm) of rain a year. Some places in the Atacama don't get a drop of rain for several years. Temperatures aren't bad, though. The long summers of coastal deserts are a pleasant 55 to 75°F (13–24°C). The short winters average a chilly but bearable 41°F (5°C).

The deserts of Nevada, Utah, and much of the western United States are semiarid deserts. These places often have huge temperature swings between day and night. You might sweat in 100°F (38°C) heat beneath a summer sun and then shiver at 50°F (10°C) beneath a starlit night sky. The cool nights help quench the thirst of plants and animals. When the temperature drops, water vapor in the air condenses on solid objects as dew. Dewdrops provide some of the moisture that plants absorb and animals drink.

And then there are the hot, dry deserts, like the Sahara. Imagine trudging through the Sahara. Do you picture yourself sweating? If you do, adjust your picture. The air is so dry that moisture evaporates from your pores before it has a chance to build up on your skin. You don't sweat.

This tree, called inflorescence of dogbane, grows in Libya.

Gear & Gadgets

THE MOST IMPORTANT GEAR on my desert adventures wasn't a super-expensive camera or anything high-tech. It was a simple, 3.2-foot (1-m) square of cloth. I wrapped it around my head and neck like a turban so it covered my nose and mouth, leaving only slits for my eyes. Called a *shemagh*, it protected my face from the intense sun and windblown sand. On cold nights, it even helped keep me warm.

In most deserts, when it rains, it pours. An entire year's worth of rain may fall in one or two brief storms. Desert plants have adapted to this rare moisture. When it rains, many plants sprout, grow, bloom, and make seeds all within a few weeks. The seeds lie in the dry soil until the next time it rains—even if it's a year or more. Then the seeds sprout and the life cycle continues.

49

PORTRAIT of the SAHARA

SUPPOSE THE ENTIRE CONTINENTAL UNITED STATES WAS A DESERT. That would be one humongous desert. Well, that's the size of the Sahara—the largest hot-weather desert in the world. It stretches across the northern third of Africa and includes about a dozen nations.

Now, let's go back to that image of you trudging through the Sahara. Put yourself there. Feel the scorching heat. Hear the howling wind. Taste the dusty air on your parched lips. What do you see around you?

Did you say sand? The Sahara certainly has its share of it, but this great desert is more than a giant sandbox. In fact, sand dunes make up less than one-fifth of the Sahara. What makes up the rest? These Sahara scenes show some of the desert's variety.

ALGERIA

MAURITANIA

S A H

MALI

>>> **ABOUT 70 KINDS** of mammals call the Sahara home, including this pair of dorcas gazelles.

>>> **PATCHES OF GREEN VEGE-TATION** mark oases, where groundwater surfaces at springs. This oasis is in the Ubari Sand Sea, Libya.

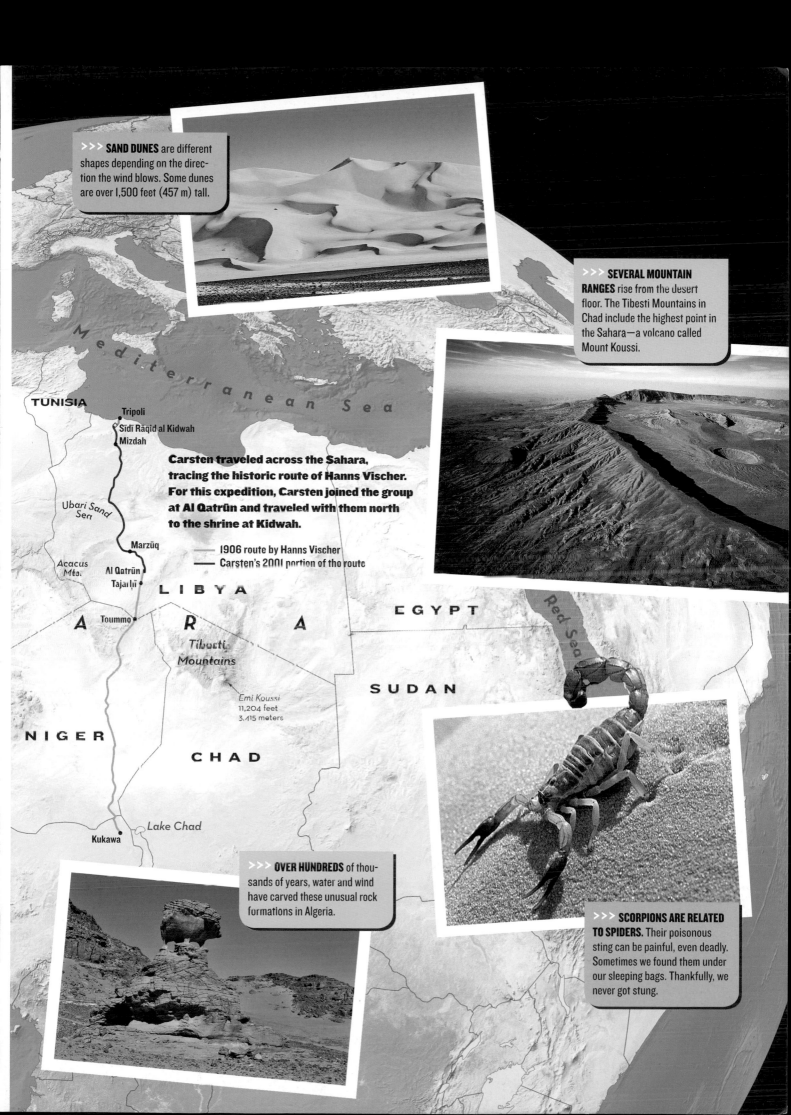

>>> **SAND DUNES** are different shapes depending on the direction the wind blows. Some dunes are over 1,500 feet (457 m) tall.

>>> **SEVERAL MOUNTAIN RANGES** rise from the desert floor. The Tibesti Mountains in Chad include the highest point in the Sahara—a volcano called Mount Koussi.

Carsten traveled across the Sahara, tracing the historic route of Hanns Vischer. For this expedition, Carsten joined the group at Al Qatrūn and traveled with them north to the shrine at Kidwah.

— 1906 route by Hanns Vischer
— Carsten's 2001 portion of the route

Mediterranean Sea

TUNISIA

Tripoli
Sīdī Rāqid al Kidwah
Mizdah

Ubari Sand Sea

Marzūq

Acacus Mts.
Al Qatrūn
Tajarḥī

LIBYA

Toummo

EGYPT

Red Sea

Tibesti Mountains

Emi Koussi
11,204 feet
3,415 meters

SUDAN

NIGER

CHAD

Lake Chad

Kukawa

>>> **OVER HUNDREDS** of thousands of years, water and wind have carved these unusual rock formations in Algeria.

>>> **SCORPIONS ARE RELATED TO SPIDERS.** Their poisonous sting can be painful, even deadly. Sometimes we found them under our sleeping bags. Thankfully, we never got stung.

Our Guide Saves THE DAY

Camel herder

WE FACE MANY DANGERS IN OUR EXPEDITIONS.

Most of the perils come from nature, like volcanic eruptions, harsh climates, and wild animals. However, in some places, danger also comes from people. The Danakil is one of those places.

We were part of a salt caravan—a long line of camels and donkeys that carry slabs of salt from mine to market. The caravans journey across the Danakil Desert in Ethiopia. This African desert is every bit as brutal as the Sahara. Yet, to the Afar people who live here, it is home.

The hard-baked Danakil provides the resources the Afar need to survive. Goatherds follow the seasonal rains and vegetation to feed their animals. Salt provides a source of income. Water holes quench a desert-size thirst.

Afar hut / Djibouti

A camel caravan / Afar, Ethiopia

NATURE'S SIGNAL

HOW DO YOU LOCATE WATER IN A DESERT?

Take your cue from wildlife. Be on the lookout for animal tracks that converge. The tracks may lead to a water hole. Notice if birds are circling in the air. A source of water may be directly below them.

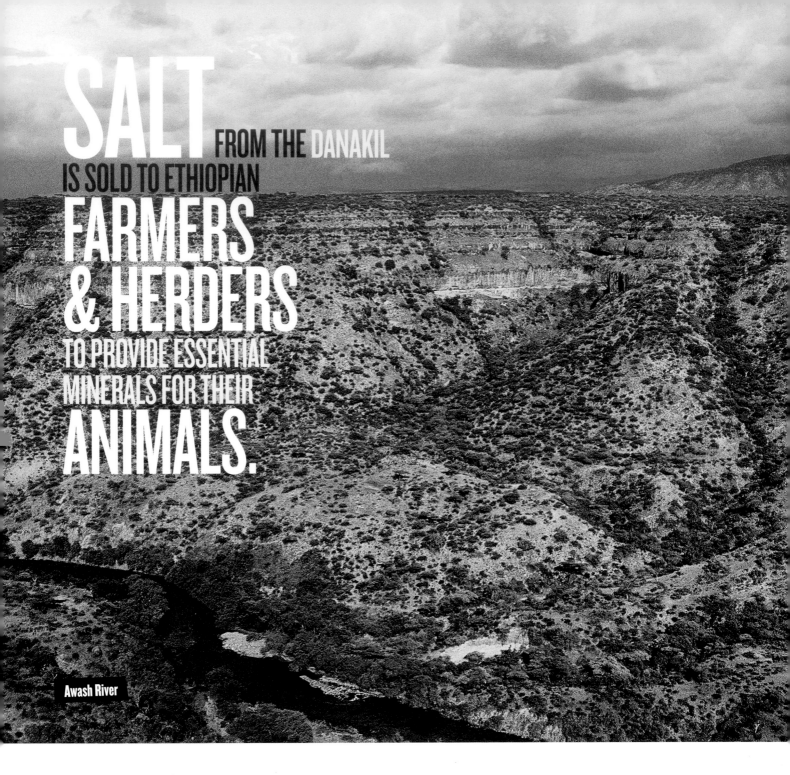

SALT FROM THE DANAKIL IS SOLD TO ETHIOPIAN FARMERS & HERDERS TO PROVIDE ESSENTIAL MINERALS FOR THEIR ANIMALS.

Awash River

The Afar fiercely protect these resources. Family groups, or clans, can be suspicious of other clans. And many were especially suspicious of non-Afar, like me. Why are you here? Are you trying to steal my goats? My salt? My water? My land?

On our expeditions, we always keep in mind that we are guests in someone's homeland. We spend months planning. That includes getting permission from governments or a local chief and finding local guides and interpreters to help us visit their lands.

The Danakil expedition was going as planned. So we were surprised to learn that our journey might be coming to a sudden end. Our guide had heard that an armed Afar group was stopping all caravans in a canyon ahead. At first, the guide said it was not safe to continue. But after we hired an additional guide, we believed they could protect us. So on we went.

We camped that night in the canyon. There was no sign of trouble. There was also no sign of other caravans. That was odd. We had expected a steady

stream of caravans passing us in the opposite direction, heading back to the mines to get more salt. Where were they?

The answer came the next afternoon. As we turned a bend, we faced hundreds of camels, donkeys, and salt merchants. The armed group had stopped several caravans for two days. They had demanded money. The ransom was paid, and the caravans were released—all at once! Suddenly they were headed toward us in a mass of people and animals.

Just as soon as we passed the crowds of people, we were stopped by the group demanding money. Our main guide— an Afar—greeted the leader. They talked. They laughed. Were they old friends? What was said? I never found out for sure, but we passed freely through the canyon and safely continued our journey.

Notes From the **Field**

RIDING A CAMEL IS FUN—FOR THE FIRST TEN MINUTES. Then the saddle and swaying can become uncomfortable. To give ourselves—and our camels—a break, we often walked. That's when I found a lot of arrowheads and ancient stone tools on the ground. It's illegal to take them, but I got some good photos.

SALT

A DESERT RESOURCE IN DANAKIL

USING THICK BRANCHES LIKE CROWBARS,

the miners pry another slab of rock-hard salt from the ground. Salt is one of the most valuable resources in the Danakil. In fact, the people call it "white gold." The miners don't have to dig underground for their white gold. It's right on the surface—thanks to the nearby Red Sea.

Over millions of years, the salty Red Sea has sometimes spilled over its shores and flooded the Danakil. The most recent flooding occurred about 30,000 years ago. The water rushed between the hills that separate the desert from the sea. Because the Danakil is hundreds of feet below sea level, the salty floodwaters poured in as if the desert were a giant bowl. Eventually the water evaporated. The salt, however, stayed behind.

Flood after flood built up layers upon layers of salt. Today the result is a huge area of hard-packed ground made of salt. Several salty lakes dot the salt plains. These lakes often flood with seasonal rains. When the floodwaters recede along the shore, they leave behind even more salt.

SALT MINING IN THE DANAKIL

>>> REMOVE

Miners use thick branches to pry large slabs from the ground.

>>> SHAPE

Miners cut the slabs and shape them into tiles. Each tile weighs between 9 and 18 pounds (4–8 kg), depending on the size.

>>> TRANSPORT

The tiles are loaded onto camels and donkeys, and the salt caravan begins. The journey usually takes three days. Then trucks carry the tiles the rest of the way to storage places.

SULFUR GAS
IN THE WATER MAKES THE HOT SPRINGS SMELL LIKE
ROTTEN EGGS.

A GEOLOGIC WONDERLAND

THERE'S NO DOUBT ABOUT IT. THE DANAKIL IS ONE HOT, DRY, DUSTY PLACE. IT'S LIKE PARTS OF THE MOON.

Yet the Danakil also has some of the most fantastic landscapes on Earth. Across a broad, white salt plain and over a brown, rocky hill lies a dazzling display of color and a chorus of sound. Hot water bubbles up in pools of lime green. Steam rises from mineral cones of lemon yellow. Small fountains spurt water from rocky formations of orange and purple. It sounds like a colorful rock garden is gargling!

This geologic wonderland is an area of hot springs. Here, water seeps through rocky underground passages. Heat from below boils the water under pressure. The water rises to the surface as gurgling pools, hissing steam, and spitting fountains called geysers. Dissolved salts and minerals separate from the water and build up colorful formations. The colors come not only from chemicals in the minerals but also from bacteria that live in the hot waters.

Where does the underground heat come from? Here's a hint: These hot springs lie in the crater of an ancient volcano! Other volcanoes are nearby too—and they're active. That means magma is close to the surface. The magma heats the rocks that heat the water that creates the hot springs.

Volcanoes in the Danakil are not surprising. This land is part of the East African Rift system. Magma wells up and drives apart sections of the cracked African plate. Millions of years from now, the Red Sea will flood the Danakil permanently. The desert will likely become part of the floor of a widening sea—a new ocean!

THE DESERT WILL LIKELY BECOME PART OF THE FLOOR OF A WIDENING SEA— A NEW OCEAN!

HOW DO DESERT PLANTS HOLD WATER?

PLANTS LOSE WATER when it evaporates from tiny holes in their leaves. Desert plants don't get much water, so they need to keep as much of it as possible. How? Let's do an experiment to find out.

>>> MATERIALS

> Water
> Paper towels
> Waxed paper
> Paper clips

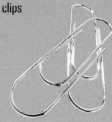

>>> STEPS

1. Wet three separate paper towels. They should be completely wet but not dripping.

2. Lay one wet paper towel on a flat surface, such as a table.

3. Roll up another wet paper towel and clip it so that it doesn't unroll. Place it on the table.

4. Lay the third wet paper towel on a piece of waxed paper of the same size. Roll up the paper towel and waxed paper together. The roll should be no looser or tighter than the second rolled paper towel. Clip the roll with the paper clips and lay it on the table.

5. After 24 hours, unroll and check the paper towels. Are any of the towels still moist? Why do you think many desert plants have a thick waxy coating on their leaves?

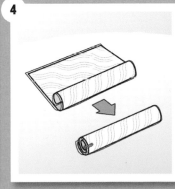

Explorers are dwarfed by giant crystals in the Cave of Crystals in Mexico.

CHAPTER 4
Caves
[Underground openings]

CAVES ARE UNLIKE ANY OTHER PLACES ON EARTH. EACH ONE IS A UNIQUE SCULPTURE CREATED BY WATER.

Water, from rain and rivers, reacts with carbon dioxide gas in the air and soil. The reaction turns the water into a weak acid. It's the same mild acid that gives soft drinks their fizz. Even though the acid is weak, it can dissolve and wear away rock, especially limestone.

It doesn't happen overnight. Acidic water seeps through the soil and reaches the limestone bedrock. The water dissolves and carries away the limestone bit by bit as it trickles through cracks in the rock. Over hundreds of thousands of years, the cracks grow into the tunnels and chambers of a cave.

Water forms a cave not only by wearing away rock but also by building it up. Water drips through cracks in the cave ceiling. A mineral called calcite, from the limestone, dissolves in the water. As the drop clings to the ceiling, the water evaporates, but a speck of calcite remains. Drop by drop, speck by speck, a rocky deposit of calcite builds downward. These deposits form into stalactites, which often look like icicles hanging from the cave ceiling.

Sometimes the drops of water fall with a little splash onto the cave floor. Then the specks of calcite build up from the floor into mounds or cones. These are stalagmites. Eventually stalactites might meet stalagmites and form columns.

An incredible variety of other cave features sprout from the floors, ceilings, and walls as water evaporates and leaves rock behind. Some features are smooth as silk; others are jagged as knives. All are among the wonders of caves.

Underground WORLDS

NATURE'S SIGNAL

HOW CAN YOU TELL IF THERE ARE ANY CAVES BENEATH YOUR FEET? Look for clues on the surface. One of the best clues is the presence of sinkholes. These are holes or craters in the ground caused by the collapse of cave ceilings.

A giant sinkhole during the dry season, Ankarana Special Reserve, northern Madagascar

LIMESTONE OUTCROP

COLUMN

LIMESTONE

STALACTITE

STALAGMITE

UNDERGROUND RIVER

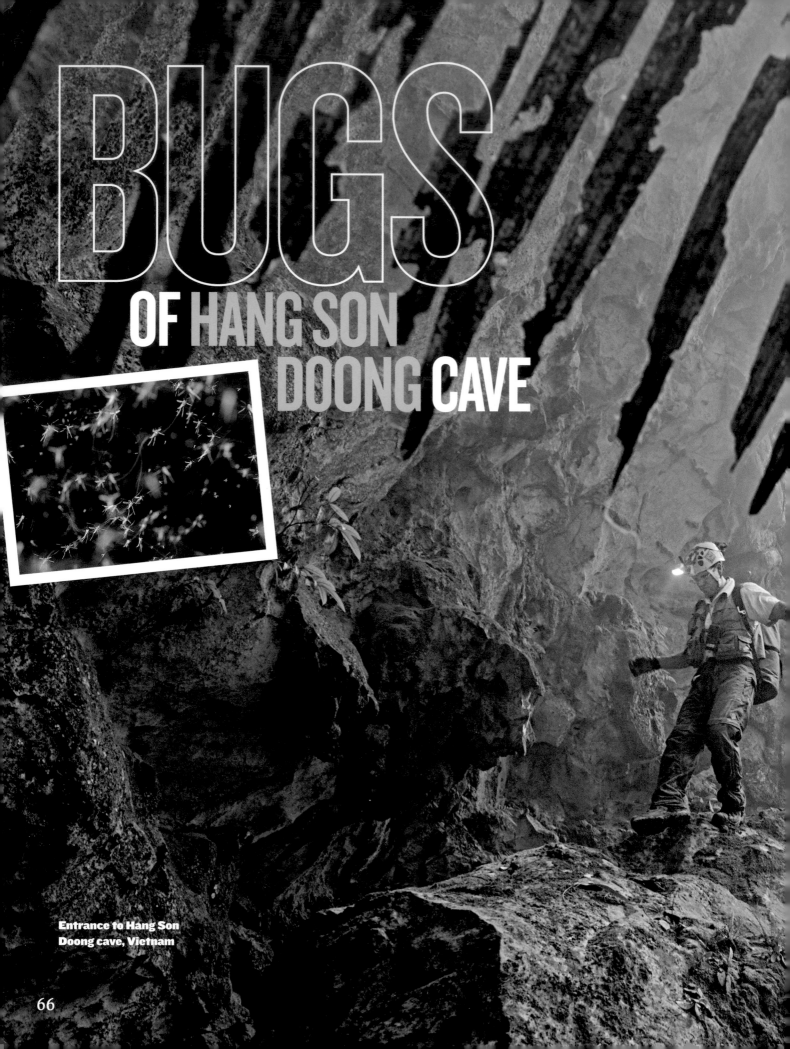

BUGS

OF HANG SON DOONG CAVE

Entrance to Hang Son
Doong cave, Vietnam

THE PAIN WAS ALMOST UNBEARABLE.

Was this little critter really going to ruin my adventure? I had survived encounters with poisonous snakes. I had slept with deadly scorpions. I had even gotten along with cranky camels. But this was one nasty experience I could have done without.

We were deep inside a cave in the Southeast Asian country of Vietnam. We were in total darkness as I tried to set up lights to see and to take some photos. Of course, lights attract insects. You may have seen a few dozen bugs fluttering around a porch light on a summer's evening. Now, multiply those few dozen by a few hundred. You get thousands of insects.

The air around my camera lights was thick with bugs. They got in my eyes, in my nose, in my mouth. I blinked away some, swallowed others, and spit out more.

Suddenly I felt something crawling in my ear. "Ah!" I yelled sharply. I jerked my head to the side, slapped at my ear, and tried to sweep out the invader with my finger. I even dunked my head under the water to drown the little guy. Nothing worked. I kept poking, but the bug was too big to turn around in my ear so instead it crawled deeper. The pressure and the pain grew. It was a horrible feeling.

Finally I called out to the expedition leader for help. I winced as he squeezed a few drops of disinfectant into my ear to kill the bug. After several anxious moments, the dead insect—a beetle—slid out of my ear. What a relief! Now I could get back to exploring one of Earth's most extreme and incredible places—Hang Son Doong cave.

Field

MOST OF A CAVE IS PITCH-BLACK. You can't see the hand in front of your face without a light. To photograph a cave's amazing features, I need to provide the right amount of light in just the right places. That's one of my greatest challenges when taking photos. To photograph the immense chambers of Hang Son Doong, I sometimes needed more than a dozen porters to hold lights. It took patience to coordinate everyone's movements but the results were worth it.

INSIDE
HANG SON DOONG

A FEW MILLION YEARS AGO, A RIVER FLOWED ALONG THE MOUNTAINOUS SURFACE IN WHAT IS NOW CENTRAL VIETNAM.

The river scoured out a valley in the limestone bedrock. But then the flowing water came upon a huge crack in the limestone. The course of the river changed as it plunged downward into the crack. River water started tunneling underground and, over time, has carved out the largest cave in the world—Hang Son Doong. The name is appropriate. It means "mountain river cave."

Today, a thick rain forest blankets the surface above Hang Son Doong. That's one reason this cave was discovered only recently. I was part of the first expedition to explore its entire length, more than 5.6 miles (9 km). Here are just a few of the surprises that awaited us.

>>> **IT TAKES A DAY** and a half of hiking through the rain forest to reach the cave entrance. One misstep on the slippery moss-covered boulders could end the journey quickly.

Gear & Gadgets

MOST OF MY ADVENTURES involve climbing, either up or down. For that, I use lots of strong nylon rope. But that's not all. First I have to fix the rope, either by tying it around a tree or rock or by connecting it to an expansion bolt that has to be securely anchored, usually by drilling it into rock. I clip a metal loop called a carabiner through a loop attached to the bolt and tie the rope to the carabiner. To descend on the rope I use a device called a descender tied to my harness. To climb up, I need two rope clamps, or ascenders. I hold one in each hand and slide them up the rope a couple feet at a time. With each motion upward, the ascenders lock in place so I don't slide back down. I can climb up steadily without fear of falling.

>>> **THIS STALAGMITE,** 15 stories tall, towers over an explorer. Another explorer half a mile away is bathed in sunlight shining through a skylight created by a collapsed cave ceiling.

>>> **A SECOND SKYLIGHT** opened up long ago when another section of the ceiling collapsed. The opening is so big that the rain forest continued to grow on the fallen rubble. The result is a rain forest growing inside the cave!

>>> **THESE ROUND ROCKS** are called cave pearls. They form as calcite from dripping water forms in layers around a grain of sand. The layers build up over centuries. Most cave pearls are the size of marbles. These are the size of softballs!

>>> **THE RIVER THAT FLOWS** through the cave is usually only a couple feet deep. During rainstorms, however, water pours into the cave and the river swells.

>>> **HOW DID WE GET** over this 200-foot (61-m) wall? The first climber drilled holes, inserted 6-inch (15-cm) screws, and connected ropes. One by one, we climbed up and over. After two weeks exploring the cave, we found a new exit.

EXPLORING
THE CAVE OF
CRYSTALS

An explorer descends into the
Cave of Crystals wearing an
orange ice-cooled suit.

UNBELIEVABLE! I KEPT MUMBLING THE WORD WITH EVERY STEP.

I had been in hundreds of caves over the years. Each one is unique and memorable, but this one was . . . unbelievable.

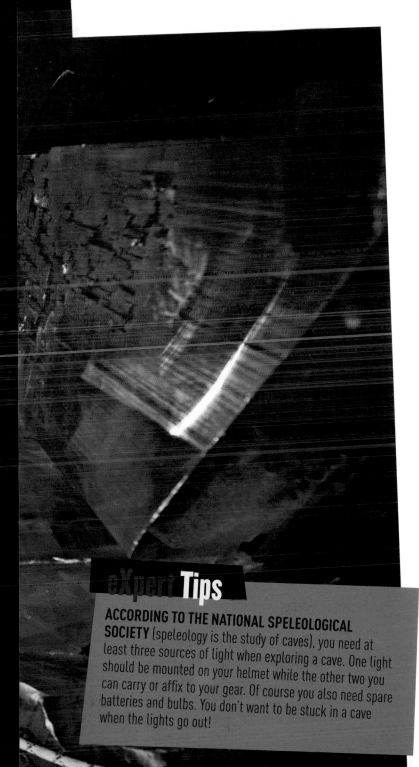

I tried comparing the cave to other things I had seen. It was like being in an ancient Greek temple that had collapsed with the pillars leaning every which way . . . sort of. Or it was like a forest that had been blown down by a volcanic eruption . . . kind of. It even looked like Superman's frozen Fortress of Solitude, with huge ice crystals jutting out of the ground . . . maybe. The fact is, I had never seen anything like this.

White gleaming crystals the size of telephone poles crisscrossed from floor to ceiling. Other crystal stumps and clumps stuck out of the walls like giant dinosaur teeth.

The crystals may look as hard as quartz but actually are one of the softest minerals known. They are crystals of selenite, which is a form of gypsum. That's the soft, chalky mineral that is ground up and pressed into drywall, or plasterboard. A metal zipper or button on clothing could scratch and chip these magnificent crystals. Even running your fingernail over them could leave a mark. Every step could damage the crystals, so we moved slowly and carefully.

The truth is we couldn't move very quickly anyway. The heat sapped so much of our energy. Unlike most caves, this one is hot— over 113°F (45°C) with nearly 100 percent humidity. That's a dangerous combination. It can lead to heatstroke quickly.

Under such conditions, you might think we'd want to explore the cave in our swimsuits. But that's no way to gear up for any kind of cave, especially this one. Sweat won't cool you down in humidity this high. Instead, we wore special vests with packs of ice sewn into them to cool our bodies. Another vest insulated the ice so that it wouldn't instantly melt. Our bright-orange caving suits added another layer of insulation as well as protection and visibility. We used masks to breathe in air cooled by ice.

Even so, we could stay in the cave for only about half an hour at a time. By then the ice was melted, and we could feel our body temperatures rising. Time to leave, for now. We cooled down in an air-conditioned tent just outside the cave. I lay there exhausted. But as soon as I recovered, I geared up for another visit inside the magical Cave of Crystals.

THE FORMATION OF THE CAVE OF CRYSTALS

IN THE YEAR 2000, TWO MINERS WERE EXPLORING A TUNNEL INSIDE A MINE IN NORTHERN MEXICO.

They were looking for rich veins of lead and silver. They found something far more unique. Nearly 1,000 feet (305 m) underground, the miners drilled through a wall of limestone. On the other side was the Cave of Crystals!

Imagine the miners' astonishment when they first laid eyes on this wonder. Crystals had been found in other caves in the area, but none this size. How did these crystals become such giants? Scientists have pieced together the answer.

About 600,000 years ago, the cave was a smooth cavity completely filled with groundwater. There were no crystals, but the water was loaded with minerals from the limestone through which it trickled. Heat from magma below the cave kept the minerals dissolved in the superheated water.

As the magma cooled, so did the water in the cave. When the water reached about 136°F (58°C), molecules of selenite started latching onto one another in a regular pattern. Molecule by molecule, crystals of selenite grew in the water. For hundreds of thousands of years, the temperature and other conditions in the cave remained the same. This allowed the crystals to keep growing, until one day in 1985.

That's when miners pumped groundwater out of the area to reach more lead and silver. They didn't realize it, but that action drained the cave. The crystals stopped growing.

AN UNCERTAIN FUTURE

TODAY A HEAVY METAL DOOR blocks the entrance to the Cave of Crystals. Explorers need permission from the mining company to enter. But the cave won't be preserved forever. When the surrounding area has been depleted of lead and silver, the mining company will move on. Then here is what will likely happen:

> PUMPS STOP
The pumps that currently keep water out of the cave will stop operating.

> CAVE FLOODS
Without the pumps, the cave will fill with groundwater.

> CRYSTALS DISSOLVE
The floodwater won't be as rich in minerals as it was before the cave's discovery. So the crystals won't continue to grow. Instead, they'll dissolve in the water.

BLUE HOLES

HOLES

THE WORLD'S MOST DANGEROUS CAVES

EVERY CAVE PRESENTS DANGERS. EXPLORERS COULD FALL AND INJURE THEMSELVES.

There's the risk of becoming trapped in tight spaces or in passages blocked by rock slides. Of course, it's also easy to get lost. But there's a type of cave with even more dangers. In the blue holes of the Bahamas you need scuba gear to swim through a layer of water filled with poisonous gas. Now *that's* a dangerous cave.

The Bahamas are islands off the southeast coast of Florida, U.S.A. These islands are famous for their clear blue waters, white sand beaches, and swaying palm trees. Less famous but more extreme are the islands' flooded caves, the blue holes of the Bahamas.

The caves formed thousands of years ago during the ice ages when Earth was much colder. At this time, more of the planet's water was frozen in glaciers. Less liquid water was available for the oceans, so sea levels dropped. That drop in sea level exposed much of the limestone that makes up the Bahamas. Caves formed. So did sinkholes. As the temperature warmed, the glaciers melted, sea levels rose, and the caves flooded.

Today, the sinkholes—nearly a thousand of them—look like ponds. But these blue holes actually are windows to worlds of beauty that few people see. The diagram on the next page shows what makes these flooded caves so special—and so dangerous.

The dark blue circle of water signals the great depth of this blue hole in Lighthouse Reef in the Bahamas.

ANATOMY OF A BLUE HOLE

>>> **WATER IN BLUE HOLES**
near the shore is salt water, like in
the sea. But away from the shore,
the water in blue holes is layered.
On top is freshwater from rainfall
and below that is salt water.

>>> **BLUE HOLES HAVE** side
passages that extend for thousands of feet. It would be easy to
get lost in these flooded tunnels.
Divers tie off and release guide
wires as they swim so they can
find their way back even if the
water gets murky. They carry
extra tanks of oxygen or leave
them at certain places along the
way. Then they won't run out of
air if they are underwater longer
than planned.

>>> **BETWEEN THE FRESH-WATER** and mixing zone, bacteria turn the water a bright orange. The bacteria produce a layer of poisonous gas called hydrogen sulfide. The gas can enter through skin to make divers itchy, dizzy, and nauseous. This can disorient divers, which is dangerous in caves, so they swim through this layer as quickly as possible.

>>> **SKELETONS OF BIRDS,** bats, and other animals lie scattered in the limestone rubble that formed when the cave ceiling collapsed long ago. Here, freshwater mixes with and salt water.

BE EARTH FRIENDLY

CAVERS HAVE A SAYING: CAVE SOFTLY. This means don't disturb the cave or any of its creatures. Unfortunately not everyone obeys this simple rule. They leave trash. Some people move carelessly through a cave and damage it. They also purposely break off stalactites as souvenirs. After being broken, the remaining piece loses color, irreversibly damaging the cave. These actions spoil the cave's beauty and damage its fragile ecosystems. If you explore a cave, move carefully. Carry out whatever you carry in, including trash. Enjoy this unique place and preserve it for others to enjoy.

TO PRESERVE THE DELICATE BEAUTY OF CAVES, CAVE SOFTLY!

HOW TO GROW STALACTITES

ROCKY FEATURES in caves take thousands of years to form. But you can model the process at home and see results in just a few days!

>>> MATERIALS

> 2 plastic cups
> Warm water
> Epsom salts
> Spoon
> Dish
> String made of cotton or wool
> 2 paper clips

>>> STEPS

1. Fill each cup with warm water. Stir Epsom salts into each cup until the salts no longer dissolve.

2. Cut about a foot (0.3 m) of string. Tie a paper clip to each end.

3. Dip the string in one of the cups to get it completely wet. Then place each end of the string into the cups. The paper clips will weigh down the string so that it stays in the cups.

4. Position the cups so that the string hangs down a bit between them. Place the dish under the string to catch any dripping.

5. Check the hanging string a couple times a day. If the string dries out, use a straw or eyedropper to add a drop of the salt solution. Try not to bump the setup. After a few days, you should see one or more stalactites growing. You might even see some stalagmites forming in the dish.

Amazing stalactites and stalagmites make this cave a marvelous space. Luray Caverns, Virginia, U.S.A.

2

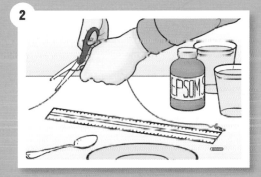

3

4

Antelope Slot Canyon / Arizona, U.S.A.

CHAPTER 5

>>> Canyons

[Narrow valleys with high, steep sides]

A WET AND WILD RIDE

IF CLIMBING MOUNTAINS IS CALLED MOUNTAINEERING, THEN WHAT IS CLIMBING CANYONS CALLED?

You guessed it—canyoneering. That's what I was doing in the Blue Mountains of Australia with other canyoneers. And that's why I was about to slide down a rope inside a waterfall.

We were near the middle of our descent down Danae Brook Canyon. High above, the brook plunged over a cliff. A high-pitched roar filled the air as the water struck the rocks around me. I checked my ropes. Then I pushed off the slippery moss-covered rocks and swung into the raging torrent.

The falling water pounded my body from all sides. It pushed me toward the rocky wall as I instantly dropped about 50 feet (15 m). I braced myself with my feet to keep from slamming into the wall. I tried to take my bearings, but not by looking up. No way was I going to look directly into the face of the thundering waterfall. I knew the force of the water could easily snap my head back and cause a terrible, even deadly, injury.

Inside the waterfall, I could barely see, so I had to move carefully. I slid down the rope, or rappelled, a short distance and landed with a splash in a shallow pool. At this point, the Danae Brook flows horizontally out toward another ledge before continuing its plunge into the canyon. I waded through the cold water, relaxed and excited at the same time. At the next ledge, I worked with my team to set up our ropes. A broad smile swept across my face as I prepared for the next leg of our wet and wild ride.

> > > **HERE THE DANAE BROOK** has cut a vertical slice through the rock. Rappelling it is like going down an elevator shaft— with a waterfall inside.

> > > **SOMETIMES THE POOLS** at the bottom of a falls are shallow enough to wade through. Other times, they are deep enough to swim through or jump into.

> > > **THERE'S STILL A WAYS TO** go, but this field of boulders is a nice spot for a lunch break. It's also a perfect place to view some of the wildlife.

Cox's River

Blue Mountains

Nepean River

Danae Brook Canyon

Sydney

Lake Burragorang

Wollondilly River

Tasman Sea

AUSTRALIA
Danae Brook Canyon

Danae Brook Canyon is about 1,200 feet (366 m) deep. But it can't be rappelled all at once. The brook falls and flows down the canyon wall in a series of steps. You can descend one step at a time. Most of the rappels are less than 100 feet (30 m).

SLICE THROUGH ROCK

DANAE BROOK CANYON IS NO ORDINARY CANYON, AND EXPLORING IT IS NO ORDINARY ADVENTURE. IT IS A SLOT CANYON AND, AS THE NAME SUGGESTS, IT IS **EXTREMELY NARROW.**

In some places, you could spread your arms and touch both canyon walls! Yet these narrow slices through rock are often more than 1,000 feet (305 m) deep. In a way, a slot canyon is like an alley between two skyscrapers—except the canyon is much more spectacular!

Because it is so narrow, a slot canyon invites you to explore up close. You can run your fingers over rocks worn smooth by the rushing water that carved the canyon. You can feel the power of the water as it flows or falls. Want to take a break? You can stop, breathe in the cool damp air, and just look and listen.

Here is how canyoneers explore a few of the other hundreds of slot canyons in Australia's Blue Mountains.

A canyoneer, below, follows a stream down a hole in Claustral Canyon. Descending into this passage felt like being swallowed by the earth.

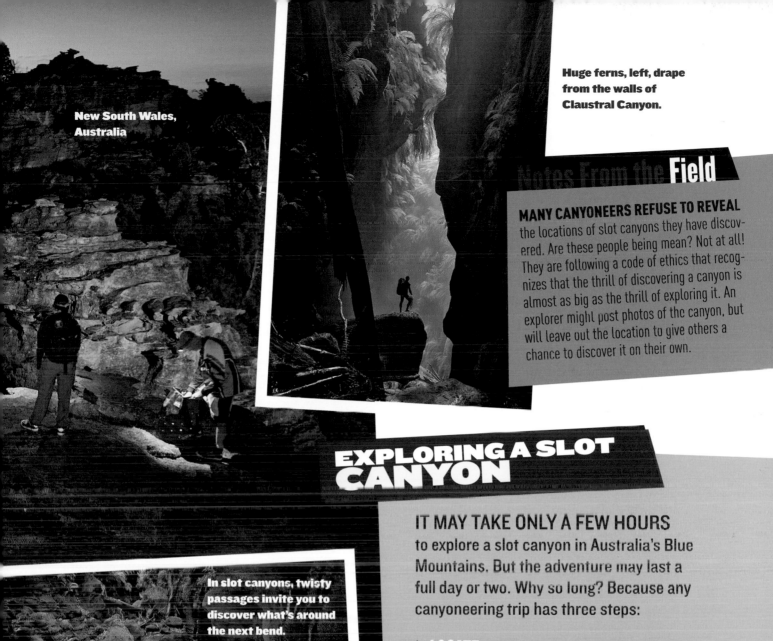

New South Wales,
Australia

Huge ferns, left, drape
from the walls of
Claustral Canyon.

MANY CANYONEERS REFUSE TO REVEAL
the locations of slot canyons they have discovered. Are these people being mean? Not at all! They are following a code of ethics that recognizes that the thrill of discovering a canyon is almost as big as the thrill of exploring it. An explorer might post photos of the canyon, but will leave out the location to give others a chance to discover it on their own.

EXPLORING A SLOT CANYON

In slot canyons, twisty passages invite you to discover what's around the next bend.

IT MAY TAKE ONLY A FEW HOURS
to explore a slot canyon in Australia's Blue Mountains. But the adventure may last a full day or two. Why so long? Because any canyoneering trip has three steps:

> ### LOCATE
Slot canyons usually are tucked away deep in the wilderness. They take hours of hiking through brush and forest to reach.

> ### DESCEND
Most canyoneers use ropes to rappel down a canyon. Others jump into deep pools. Some parts of the descent may include swimming across ponds or rivers, wading through streams, and hiking across boulders and down gentler slopes.

> ### ASCEND
After you reach the bottom of the canyon, then what? Right, you have to climb back up. Canyoneers might camp overnight and begin the grueling climb in the morning. Usually they follow the canyon until they come to steep slopes that they can hike up.

It's a tight
squeeze when
the canyon
walls almost
meet in Tiger
Snake Canyon.

85

SLOT CANYONS
OF THE SOUTHWEST UNITED STATES

SOME OF THE
MOST BEAUTIFUL
SLOT CANYONS IN THE WORLD
HAVE FORMED IN THE SOUTH-
WESTERN UNITED STATES.

One of the most famous is Antelope Canyon in Arizona. Like many slot canyons of the arid Southwest, Antelope Canyon has no permanent stream. Water flows only during rains. So exploring this canyon is usually an easy hike.

If you want to get your feet wet, try the Narrows in Zion National Park, Utah. Here, canyon walls rise more than 1,500 feet (457 m) from a shallow river that is sometimes only 20 feet (6 m) wide. The views are awesome. It's a tough hike, though. The water level varies from ankle deep to waist deep. A sturdy walking stick helps keep you from falling on the smooth slippery rocks that form the river bottom.

LEFT: These hikers are in the midst of a 16-mile (26-km) trek through the Narrows—the longest slot canyon in the world.

BELOW: A narrow path weaves through the Escalante slot canyons in Utah, U.S.A.

Gear & Gadgets

GLOBAL POSITIONING SYSTEM (GPS) devices use satellite signals to find location and height above sea level. I always take my GPS unit with me on expeditions. It doesn't work well in most slot canyons because the steep walls and overhanging rock block the signals. But it helps me find my way to and from the canyons, especially in remote areas. However, don't forget paper maps, too, because they are more helpful than a GPS in canyons.

The colorful layers of sandstone in Antelope Canyon look like they were painted on. The colors shift with the changing sunlight.

87

CANYON DANGERS

IF YOU POUR A CUP OF WATER ONTO A BAKING SHEET, THE WATER SPREADS OUT AND BARELY COVERS THE SHEET.

But if you pour that same amount of water into a small narrow glass, the glass may fill completely. Flash floods, one of the greatest dangers of exploring slot canyons, work in a similar way.

> HEED THE FORECAST

Flash floods happen when rainwater floods an area quickly. Even if a storm is many miles away, slopes and gullies can quickly funnel a lot of water from the surrounding land into a slot canyon. Because the canyon is so narrow, water levels can rise over your head in a matter of seconds. Or a wall of water can come rushing down the canyon all at once. If the forecast calls for rain anywhere in the area, save your canyon adventure for another day.

> WATCH YOUR STEP

Hiking in a canyon isn't like strolling down the sidewalk. Smooth rocks covered with moss or algae can be as slippery as ice. Broken, jagged rocks can be even more treacherous. If you walk in a stream, the swift current can knock you off balance even if the water is only ankle deep.

To help keep a broken bone or sprained ankle from ending your adventure, wear sturdy hiking boots, even in a stream. A walking stick helps you stay balanced. And don't forget common sense. Running and jumping are great ways to stay healthy, but not in a rocky canyon. Tread carefully.

> DRESS FOR THE TRIP

Even in summer, slot canyons tend to be cool. And the streams tend to be cold. Add in a gentle breeze, and your body temperature can drop to dangerous levels. When your body temperature drops too much, you can get sick. This condition is called hypothermia. To avoid hypothermia, dry clothing should be in any canyoneer's waterproof backpack.

NATURE'S SIGNAL

THE WEATHER FORECAST SAID CLEAR SKIES. It's a beautiful day to explore a slot canyon. But forecasts are not always correct, and the weather can change quickly. According to the U.S. National Park Service, any of these conditions can signal a possible flash flood in canyons:

- Build up of clouds
- Sound of distant thunder
- Sudden change of stream water from clear to muddy
- Sudden appearance of twigs and leaves in water
- Rising water levels or stronger current
- Increasing sound of roaring water in distance

CARSTEN'S BIRD'S-EYE VIEW
OF CANYONS IN CHINA

THE CONDITIONS COULD NOT BE BETTER.

The wind was light. The air was clear. It was perfect for the second flight of our multicopter-cam. This remote-controlled device flies like a helicopter. It carries video cameras and still-photo cameras to provide a bird's-eye view of Earth's extreme places.

We were using the multicopter-cam to get images of the incredible Enshi Grand Canyon in southern China. Here, fantastic limestone towers reach to the sky. The copter-cam allowed us to capture their majesty in a way like no other.

And that's what we were doing ... for the first five minutes of the flight. I was controlling the cameras while the multicopter-cam's engineer was controlling the actual flight. All of a sudden the device started to wobble. It wouldn't respond to our controls. My heart sank as we watched this fantastic piece of technology crash into the forest at the bottom of the canyon.

Our photo and video expedition had just become a rescue mission. We saw the general area where the copter-cam went down. So I hiked into the canyon to find it. Other members of the team stayed up on the canyon wall where they could direct me by using our radios. I picked my way through brush, ferns, and roots on the forest floor. Then suddenly, by the side of a downed tree, I saw it.

"I found the copter! I found the copter!" I reported.

"That's awesome," came the reply.

I peered closer. "But it doesn't look awesome."

What a mess. Three of the six arms were broken. Cables were torn apart. The landing gear was busted. Other parts were heavily damaged, and the camera itself was missing. I carefully untangled the wreckage, located the camera, and carried it back. I was frustrated. Would our copter-cam fly again before we had to leave this magnificent canyon?

Yes! The engineer was able to repair it. We lost a lot of time but were able to complete 20 more flights throughout the canyon. Our mission was a success.

expert Tips

THE AMERICAN RED CROSS RECOMMENDS that you take a first aid kit on any outdoor adventure. Here are some items to include:

- gauze pads
- adhesive bandages
- antiseptic solution
- cloth tape
- elastic bandages
- tweezers
- mirror
- alcohol swabs
- dishwashing soap
- latex gloves
- antihistamine (for allergic reactions)
- pain reliever

HOW TO USE A TOPOGRAPHIC MAP

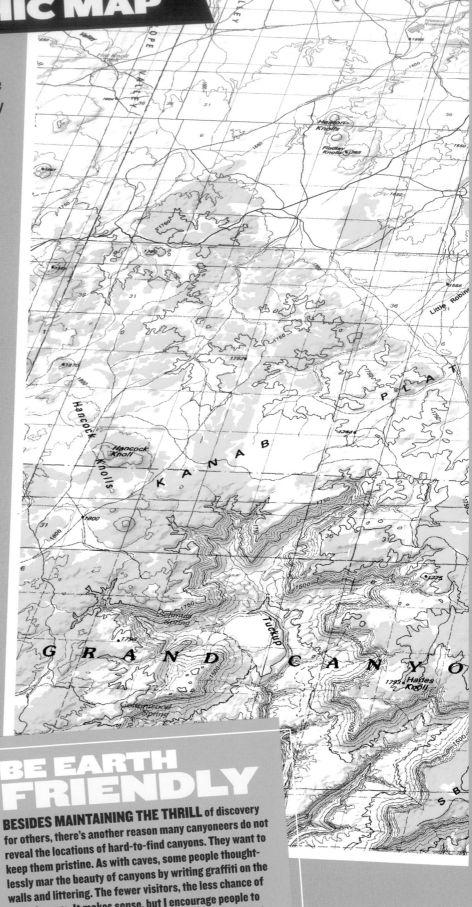

WHETHER PLANNING an adventure in canyon country, a deep forest, or any other wilderness, the best guide you can have is a topographic map of the area. These maps show the shape of the land—the topography.

Look at this topographic map. See all those brown squiggly lines? Those are contour lines. Each one connects points of equal elevation, or the height above sea level. How? Well, imagine being on the side of a hill. Instead of walking up or down the hill, you walk around the hill, always at the same elevation. You would be tracing a contour line.

Topographic maps are easy and fun to read. Just remember these tips:

> A series of closed contour lines, or loops inside one another, shows a hill.

> Where contour lines are far apart, the land slopes gently. Where the lines are close together, the land slopes steeply, like at a canyon.

> The contour interval is the vertical distance between contour lines. The interval is marked on the map. Some maps have an interval of only 10 or 20 feet (3 or 6 m). Others have an interval of 50 or 100 feet (15 or 30 m). Only every fifth contour line is marked with its elevation.

> Exact elevations are marked by the numbers next to tiny black dots.

With a little practice, you'll be able to see the lay of the land just by looking at the map. Start with the map shown here. See if you can answer these questions:

1. Where is the main canyon? Trace it with your finger.

2. Find a hill. What is its elevation?

3. Can you find a canyon with a steep slope? What about one with a gentle slope?

BE EARTH FRIENDLY

BESIDES MAINTAINING THE THRILL of discovery for others, there's another reason many canyoneers do not reveal the locations of hard-to-find canyons. They want to keep them pristine. As with caves, some people thoughtlessly mar the beauty of canyons by writing graffiti on the walls and littering. The fewer visitors, the less chance of such damage. It makes sense, but I encourage people to explore and enjoy Earth's wild places. Just do so without leaving a trace.

CHAPTER 6

>>> Extreme Forces

X

[Tornado—A quickly spinning column of air that stretches from the ground to the clouds; Lightning—A flash of light caused by electricity passing between clouds or between clouds and the ground]

A tornado rampages through a field near Manchester, South Dakota, U.S.A.

CHASING TORNADOES

"CARSTEN, LET'S GO! WE HAVE TO GET OUT OF HERE!"

"Yeah, yeah," I thought. "Just one more photo."

I pointed my camera at the whirling monster bearing down on us and clicked off another shot. Then another. Maybe just one more...

"Carsten! Now!"

I jumped into the car and we sped off. I looked back at the tornado. It was incredible being so close to such a force. I had almost given up hope of ever experiencing it.

For three spring seasons in a row, my fellow storm chasers and I had been crisscrossing the central plains of the United States in search of tornadoes. Why? To better understand them.

I had journeyed far and wide to explore Earth's most amazing places and experience its most powerful forces. I had come to understand and respect the forces that blast lava from a volcano, carve out caves in a glacier, and shape our world in magnificent ways. But now I was in the middle of wheat fields and prairies. These seem like ordinary places but they are subject to some of the most extraordinary forces on Earth—tornadoes. Like the scientists I accompanied,

I wanted to understand these forces. If we know more about when, where, and how tornadoes form and how they act, we can provide more accurate warnings and save lives. That's what we were trying to do. But first we had to find these whirlwinds.

Our vehicles were equipped with the latest technology—radar, satellite imagery, GPS—everything we needed to track the supercell thunderstorms that might produce tornadoes. So far we had struck out.

Oh sure, we had felt the fury of many storms. Sheets of rain had blinded us. Violent winds had rocked us. Pounding hail had bombarded us. But we had seen only two tornadoes, and before we could get close enough to study them, they had fizzled out.

All of that changed on our last day of storm chasing for the season. It was Tuesday, June 24, 2003. In South Dakota, U.S.A., it became known as Tornado Tuesday. Between 5:00 p.m. and 11:00 p.m. 67 tornadoes tore across the South Dakota prairie. The worst of them was now hot on our trail.

"NOW WE WEREN'T CHASING THE TORNADO. THE TORNADO WAS CHASING US!"

Expedition leader Tim Samaras plants a tornado probe, called a "turtle," in the path of an approaching tornado near Woonsocket, South Dakota, U.S.A.

The twister was huge—half a mile (0.8 km) wide. It had just destroyed a small farm community called Manchester. I saw it happen. In a few seconds, every structure completely blew apart. I finally understood the power of tornadoes.

Suddenly the car skidded to a stop. The leader of the expedition, Tim Samaras, jumped out to place a bright red metal object on the side of the road. Hopefully the tornado would sweep right over it. Sensors inside the red probe would then measure wind speed, air pressure, and other vital signs of the twister.

"We don't have time!" someone shouted.

The scientist quickly set down the probe and glanced at the twister only a few hundred yards away. He ran back to the car, flew down the road a few seconds, and left another probe. By the time he placed the third probe the twister had reached the first. A direct hit! Would the tornado give up any of its secrets? We were anxious to retrieve the probe and find out.

TORNADO POWER

WEATHER DOESN'T GET MORE EXTREME THAN TORNADOES.

Many people think they are the most dangerous and frightening of all weather events. The residents of Manchester, South Dakota, U.S.A., certainly would agree. So would those in Parkersburg, Iowa, U.S.A.

On May 25, 2008, a powerful tornado slammed Parkersburg. Winds of more than 200 miles an hour (322 km/h) uprooted trees, swept away homes, and tossed cars like toys. Concrete floors and brick walls were pulverized into bits and pieces. Steel girders were twisted like taffy. Seven people died and hundreds more lost nearly everything.

Parkersburg wasn't alone. During that last week of May, storms raged all across the Great Plains. This area is known as Tornado Alley because tornadoes occur there most frequently. And frequent they were! At least 235 twisters scarred the countryside that week.

Tornadoes can occur any time of the year, but spring is prime time in the United States. That's when warm moist air often moves north from the Gulf of Mexico as cold dry air blows east over the Rocky Mountains. The different air masses clash over the Great Plains, forming violent thunderstorms that sometimes spawn tornadoes.

Joplin, Missouri, U.S.A. / 2011

THE TORNADO was on the ground for 38 terrifying minutes. It chewed up 22 miles (35 km) of land and most anything that stood in its way. Gaining strength along its path, it grew to a mile wide. A twister that big doesn't have the typical shape of an elephant's trunk. Instead, it looks like a wedge sweeping across the horizon. Several smaller tornadoes spun along the edge of the larger whirlwind, like tops spinning on a superfast merry-go-round. The combined effect of these winds was devastating. Vehicles were thrown into homes or wrapped around trees. Frame houses were reduced to wood chips. Structures of concrete and steel were flattened. In the town of 2,000, nearly 160 people lost their lives and more than 1,000 suffered injuries.

Parkersburg, Iowa, U.S.A. / 2008

El Reno, Oklahoma, U.S.A. / 2013

AVIATION TECHNOLOGY

N5185F

IF IT'S DIFFICULT TO PICTURE a roaring twister a mile (1.6 km) wide, then one that is 2.6 miles (4.2 km) wide may be unimaginable. Yet that's the size of the tornado—the largest on record—that struck near El Reno, Oklahoma, U.S.A. Estimated wind speeds reached almost 300 miles an hour (483 km/h). That's nearly a record, too. The tornado tore through farms and fields. Its sudden changes of direction and strength made it extremely dangerous. This unpredictable behavior caught my dear friends and colleagues in its deadly winds. The impact this storm had on my life is immeasurable.

Gear & Gadgets

THE RED PROBES PLACED IN A TORNADO'S PATH ARE CALLED "TURTLES." You can see why. The probe looks a bit like a turtle's shell. It's a perfect design. The flat cone shape prevents the tornado from lifting it and destroying the sensors inside. These sensors measure wind speed and direction, air pressure, temperature, and humidity. One of the turtles at the Manchester tornado measured the biggest drop in air pressure ever recorded.

Some turtles have video cameras inside. They're called "media probes." One of these probes recorded close to a direct hit. The center of the tornado was so close! The camera took shots to show us what it's like inside a tornado. Talk about extreme!

AFTER DISASTER STRIKES

An elderly woman bent down to pick up a framed photograph. The glass plate covering the photo was shattered. So was her life.

It is heartbreaking to see people sifting through a pile of rubble that used to be their home. They have lost everything to a tornado. Yet when I talk to them, the message is almost always the same: "We will rebuild."

Parkersburg, Iowa, sent that message loud and clear. After the 2008 tornado destroyed a third of the town, the cleanup and rebuilding started immediately. The Federal Emergency Management Agency (FEMA) and other government agencies provided much of the funding needed. But it was the townspeople and thousands of volunteers from nearby communities who provided the helping hands. Within a year the high school was rebuilt. Within three years the only sign of the tornado's path was the lack of large trees.

The people of Joplin, Missouri, U.S.A., pulled together, too. Three years after their devastating 2011 twister, 90 percent of the destroyed homes had been rebuilt. The town also showed it was back in business. About 450 of the 500 stores, factories, and other damaged businesses had reopened. What's more, 150 new businesses had opened.

Like Parkersburg, the residents of Joplin have rebuilt with safety in mind. More basements are reinforced with concrete. Storm shelters are stronger. Sewer systems have been repaired and emergency plans have been updated. These and other improvements will prove helpful the next time Earth's most extreme winds strike.

HOW TORNADOES FORM

Here's a general idea of how we think tornadoes form.

STEP 1

> Winds either blow in different directions and altitudes, or at different speeds (as shown below), to create a sheer face and cause a horizontal tube of air to spin within a thunderstorm.

STEP 2

> Strong currents of rising warm air, or updrafts, tilt the spinning tube of air upright. Continued strong updrafts make the column of air spin faster. This lowers the air pressure inside the column creating a thunderstorm. If it rotates, this is called a supercell. Because air moves from high to low pressure, the low pressure in the spinning column sucks in nearby air like a giant whirling vacuum cleaner. Supercells are the monsters of thunderstorms.

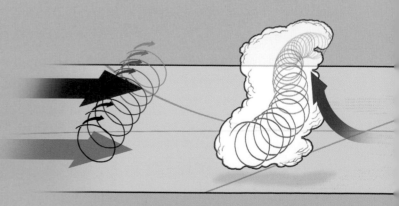

People enjoy an arts festival (above) after Joplin, Missouri, U.S.A., was rebuilt.

Damage (left) from a catastrophic hurricane in Joplin.

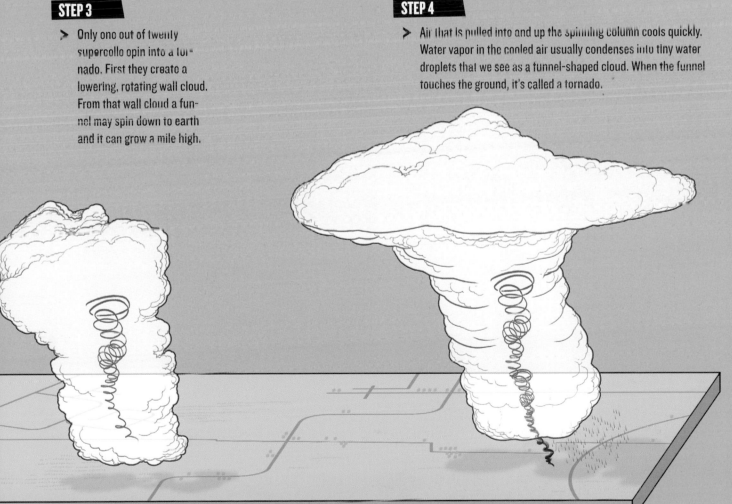

STEP 3

> Only one out of twenty supercells spin into a tornado. First they create a lowering, rotating wall cloud. From that wall cloud a funnel may spin down to earth and it can grow a mile high.

STEP 4

> Air that is pulled into and up the spinning column cools quickly. Water vapor in the cooled air usually condenses into tiny water droplets that we see as a funnel-shaped cloud. When the funnel touches the ground, it's called a tornado.

CAPTURING LIGHTNING

I COULD ALMOST FEEL THE ELECTRICITY IN THE AIR. MAYBE IT WAS JUST THE EXCITEMENT.

It was late summer, and once again we were on the wide-open plains. Another monster storm was bearing down on us. A few rays from the setting sun lit the bottom of the massive gray clouds, giving the whole scene an eerie glow. The cameras were rolling. Everyone was filled with anticipation of "the show."

Suddenly the sky in front of us came alive with lightning. Each blinding bolt of electricity was followed by a deafening *ka-BOOM!* Above the roaring thunder, we shouted, "Whoa!" "Beautiful!" "Did you see that?"

We saw it all right. We were just hoping the cameras saw it, because there's a lot more to lightning than meets the eye.

That thought occurred to me as I quickly snapped images of the fantastic lightning show. I knew that my photos could show only part of lightning's short but incredible journey. That's because a lightning bolt between a storm cloud and the ground begins as a dim spark. The spark is a stream of negatively charged electricity that zigzags its way from the cloud toward the ground. This stream of charge is called a stepped leader. As the stepped leader nears the ground, a stream of positive charge reaches up to meet it. When the two connect . . . FLASH! A brilliant burst of electricity rushes up the completed path. This return stroke is what we see as lightning.

FOLLOW LIGHTNING'S journey between cloud and ground.

STEP 1

> A stream of negative charge, called a stepped leader, starts forking its way from the cloud toward the ground. The stepped leader is too fast to see with the naked eye.

STEP 2

> Positive charge builds along the ground and is attracted to the negative charge coming down from the cloud. When the negative charge gets close enough, streamers of positive charge leap up to meet it. This is called a dart.

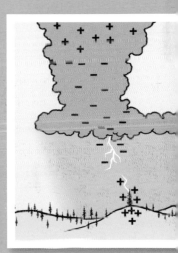

STEP 3

> The charges meet in a brilliant flash. Electricity rushes up the path toward the cloud, creating the bright light we see as lightning. The entire process lasts about one-fifth of a second.

NATURE'S SIGNAL

IF YOU ARE OUTSIDE WHILE A STORM IS BREWING and your hair stands up, get inside immediately. Your flyaway hair could be a sign that lightning is about to strike. Positive charges may be rising from your body. You don't want to be there if a stepped leader is about to descend. If you wait for the strike, you'll be too late. The lightning is faster than you can react.

THE NEED FOR SPEED

IN ADDITION TO MY STILL-PHOTO CAMERAS, WE WERE USING TWO HIGH-SPEED VIDEO CAMERAS.

How fast do these cameras run? Well, a typical home video camera may shoot 30 frames per second. At this speed, you can record and play back anything that happens no faster than $^1/_{30}$ of a second. That's fine for birthday parties, sporting events, and even Hollywood movies. But it's way too slow if you want to unveil the mysteries of lightning. A stepped leader makes its way from cloud to ground in just a few thousandths of a second. No problem. We had obtained special video cameras that run at a speedy 10,000 frames per second!

Tim Samaras, the leader of our tornado and lightning chases, had used these cameras before. When he played back the slow-motion video of his first "captured" lightning strike, everyone was blown away. For the first time in history, we could see the initial spark peeking out from a cloud, branching off, and zigzagging to earth. The video also shows the barely visible streamers reaching up.

We still can't see lightning's entire journey. Even the high-speed cameras are too slow to show any detail of the instant the stepped leader meets the upward streamers. What exactly happens in that first blinding flash? No one knows. But we have a way to find out. Enter the Kahuna.

That's the nickname of an ultra-high-speed video camera. The Kahuna is actually a combination of 82 smaller cameras arranged in a huge circle. A superfast spinning mirror in the center sweeps light across the cameras. This lets the Kahuna record at almost a walloping 1.4 million frames per second! That's the kind of speed we need.

Back on the plains, the storm raged. Tim hopped into the trailer that houses the 1,600-pound (725-kg) Kahuna. He started the engine that makes the mirror spin. It took ten seconds to get up to speed. Meanwhile lightning flashed one after another. In a minute, the engine would have to be shut down to keep from overheating. Would he choose the right moment? It is a technical challenge that takes split-second timing, knowledge, and a lot of luck.

Luck wasn't with us this time. But there are lots of storms every summer. Maybe with some improvements to the Kahuna, and a little more luck, we'll finally see one of nature's most extreme displays.

Tips

THE NATIONAL OCEANIC AND ATMOSPHERIC ADMINISTRATION (NOAA) has a simple rule about lightning safety: When thunder roars, go indoors! It's a good rule. The intense heat from a lighting bolt produces a sound wave that you hear as thunder. So if thunder is in the area, lightning is, too. NOAA recommends that you stay indoors at least 30 minutes after the last rumble of thunder.

What about researchers like us who chase storms? There's no doubt we take certain risks. But we are not reckless. We are well-trained professionals and have studied these forces for decades. We stay in our vehicles as much as possible. We keep our distance from trees or other tall objects that might attract a lightning strike. We stay away from wire fences and other metal items that conduct electricity. And if the storm gets too close to us, we move.

Notes From the Field

TIM SAMARAS DESIGNED THE TURTLE PROBES, the Kahuna, and other instruments to measure weather events. I was lucky enough to accompany this extraordinary engineer and scientist as we chased storms. We shared a passion for unlocking their secrets. Sadly Tim, along with his son Paul and fellow researcher Carl Young, were killed in the El Reno tornado in 2013. Like all researchers who chase storms, they knew the dangers. They also knew that the more we learn about storms, the safer it will make us all. This pursuit of knowledge and desire to help people was their true passion.

HOW TO MAKE A TORNADO IN A BOTTLE

A TORNADO IS A KIND OF VORTEX. If you have ever watched water drain from a sink or bathtub, you have seen another kind of vortex. It's the whirlpool that forms right above the drain. In both cases, a fluid (air or liquid) swirls around and around pulling in more fluid from nearby. You can make a liquid vortex that acts much like a tornado. Gather these materials:

>>> MATERIALS

- Two empty 2-liter plastic soda bottles
- Metal washer, about 1 inch (2.5 cm) in diameter with a $^3/_8$-inch (1-cm) diameter hole
- Electrical tape or duct tape
- Dishwashing detergent
- Food coloring
- Glitter

>>> STEPS

1. Wash off the labels on the bottles so you get a nice clear view.

2. Fill one of the bottles about two-thirds full with water.

3. Add a few drops of dishwashing detergent and food coloring. Then add a couple pinches of glitter.

4. Place the empty bottle on top of the filled one, opening to opening, with the washer between them. Tape the bottles together so that water won't leak when you turn them over.

5. Turn the bottles over so that the one with water is on top. Give the bottles a few quick horizontal rotations. Then watch a vortex form in the top bottle as the water drains. The glitter will help you see how the spinning motion pulls water into the vortex. After the water drains you can turn the bottles over and make another vortex. How is your water vortex like a tornado? How is it different?

CONCLUSION

THIS BOOK HAS TAKEN US on some incredible adventures. I hope you have enjoyed reading about them as much as I've enjoyed sharing them.

Think back. If you could have come along with me on any one of these adventures, which would it have been? What was special about that expedition? Then skim through the book. Which photos are your favorites? What information in each chapter was the most surprising? What fun facts would you most like to share with others? Go ahead and share them.

This book is filled with the thrills of exploration. But the book is just a start. Even more thrills await you beyond these pages—in the great outdoors. That's where the real fun and excitement of exploring comes in. Maybe on a vacation you'll have the opportunity to visit a place you've never been before. Sounds like the perfect time to turn off your electronics and get out and explore our natural world. I hope this book has inspired you to do that.

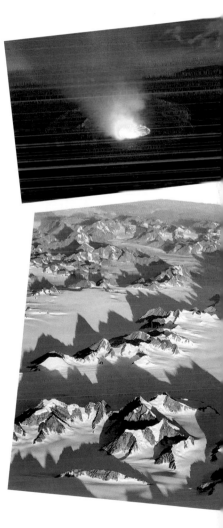

You don't have to go to faraway places, either. There's a lot to explore in your own community. Most areas have nature centers that set aside land for people of all ages to explore and learn about. You'll discover interesting facts about the plants and animals that live there. You'll learn what the area was like before people settled there and what forces shaped the landscape.

You can also explore the natural areas in your own neighborhood. Try to identify the trees and other plants. The library has guidebooks that will help you do that. Watch the animals, too. Observe what they look like and how they act. Be careful, though. Keep your distance from animals. Only go places where you have permission to go, and explore new places with an adult, especially far from home.

I'll be exploring too. In fact, as you read this, I might be off on another expedition. I may be climbing a steaming volcano, squeezing through a tight spot in a cave, or wiping frost off my goggles on a glacier. It won't all be extreme, though. I enjoy weekend hikes in the woods near my home. And I can spend an hour just watching squirrels chase each other up and down trees or bees buzzing in a garden.

So, let's explore our world together. The more we learn about it, the more we'll appreciate its beauty and wonder. And the more we'll care about it and care about protecting it from harm. After all, this entire planet—from the mild to the extreme—is home to all of us.

GLOSSARY

Acid A chemical substance, it can wear away rock and other solids

Acid pools Pools of water with dangerous chemicals that can wear away solids, including rock and metal

Andesitic lava Lava of medium hotness and speed of flow

Antarctic Circle An imaginary line that encircles the south polar region. On the first day of summer in the Northern Hemisphere, every location between the Antarctic Circle and the South Pole has 24 hours of darkness.

Arctic Circle An imaginary line that encircles the north polar region. On the first day of summer in the Northern Hemisphere, every location between the Arctic Circle and the North Pole has 24 hours of daylight.

Ascender A device used to ascend, or climb up, on a rope

Calcite A mineral found in limestone

Carabiner A metal loop through which a rope is connected for climbing

Carbon dioxide A colorless, odorless gas that is in the air and in lava and volcanoes; can be dangerous in large amounts

Canyon A narrow valley with high steep sides

Canyoneering The exploration of canyons

Cave An underground chamber

Condense To change from a gas into a liquid

Contour line A line on a map that connects all points of equal elevation, or height

Crampons Metal spikes placed on boots to keep from slipping

Crater A bowl-shaped area that forms around the central opening in a volcano

Crust The solid rocky layer that covers Earth, both on land and on the ocean floor

Descender A device used to descend, or climb down, on a rope

Desert A place that receives less than ten inches (25.4 cm) of rainfall per year

Elevation Height above sea level

Energy efficient Using as little energy as possible to operate

Eruption When lava, gases, and solid rock emerge from a volcano to the surface

Expedition A journey to explore and gather information about an area or event

Extremophiles Microbes that thrive in extreme conditions, such as places with high heat or toxic gases

Evaporate To change from a liquid into a gas

Felsic lava A cooler lava; of all lavas, it flows the slowest

Geyser An opening in the ground that shoots hot water and steam into the air

Glacier A large mass of ice that slowly moves downhill

Groundwater Water that moves and collects underground

Gypsum A very soft mineral

Hydrogen sulfide A poisonous gas

Hypothermia A condition in which body temperature drops to dangerous levels, preventing body parts from working

Ice age A period of time when temperatures drop and glaciers form over much of the land

Ice sheet A huge mass of ice that covers a wide area of land

Lava flow The area of land covered by lava as it flows out of a volcano

Lethal Deadly

Lightning Flash of electric spark passing between clouds or between clouds and ground

Limestone A kind of rock that dissolves easily in carbonated water and forms most caves

Mafic lava The hottest lava; it flows the fastest of all lavas

Magma A mixture of melted rock, gases, and water underground

Meltwater Liquid water formed by the melting of ice

Methane A colorless, odorless, and dangerous gas; can be burned to produce electricity

Microbes Life-forms too small to see except through a microscope

Multicopter-cam A remote-controlled multirotor (like a helicopter) with cameras attached for taking video and photographs

Plate boundaries The edges of the pieces of the Earth's crust that form the solid outer layer of the planet

Precipitation Water that falls to Earth's surface, either as liquid (rain) or solid (snow, hail)

Predators Animals that hunt other animals for food

Prediction A forecast or telling of future events

RESOURCES
& FURTHER READING

Rappel A way of climbing down a cliff using a rope attached at the top of the cliff

Quartz A very hard mineral found in many kinds of rocks

Ring of Fire The belt of volcanoes and earthquakes that form a rim around the Pacific Ocean

Semiarid A place that gets very little rainfall

Shaft A deep vertical (up-and-down) passage

Shemagh A piece of cloth, like a scarf, worn wrapped around the head and neck

Sinkhole An opening in the ground that forms when the roof of a cave collapses

Slot canyon A very narrow canyon with high walls

Spatter cone The wall of solid rock that forms a volcanic vent as the spattering lava cools and hardens

Speleology The study of caves

Stalactites Rock formations that hang like icicles from the roof of a cave

Stalagmites Rock formations that build up like cones from the floor of a cave

Stepped leader A stair-like electric discharge that is the beginning of a lightning strike

Sulfur A yellow element that is often part of the gases in volcanoes; smells like rotten eggs

Supercell A strong thunderstorm with rotating winds

Topographic map A map that shows the shape of the land

Topography The shape of the land

Tornado A rapidly spinning column of air that stretches from the ground to the clouds

Turtle probe A metal cone filled with sensors that measure a tornado that passes over it

Vent Passageway in a volcano through which gases and lava flow

Volcano An opening in Earth's crust from which gases and melted rock spill onto the surface

Volcanologist A scientist who studies volcanoes

Volcanology The study of volcanoes

THERE ARE LOTS OF OTHER WAYS TO EXPLORE OUR EXTREME PLANET:

> The Internet is your doorway to all sorts of information, games, and videos about nature's wonders. You can start your explorations at kids.earth.nasa.gov. It's full of activities and information about Earth's air, land, and water.

> One way to explore Earth's natural wonders is to explore national parks. You can start at the world's first national park—Yellowstone. Here's a link to all kinds of games and other fun at Yellowstone, including a scavenger hunt: nps.gov/yell/learn/kidsyouth/parkfun.htm.

> Do you remember reading about the probe that recorded a direct hit from a tornado? Here's the video from inside that probe: ngm.nationalgeographic.com/2005/06/inside-tornadoes/video-interactive.

> And if you're into extreme weather, don't pass up this site: nws.noaa.gov/om/reachout/kidspage.shtml.

> Check out Carsten's website for more adventures: carstenpeter.com.

> Of course, National Geographic has tons of fun and interesting videos, photos, and even more books on weather you should check out: kids.national geographic.com.

INDEX

PHOTO CREDITS

READY TO ROCK?

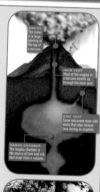

Explore the wild and wondrous world UNDER your feet with geologist Steve Tomecek, aka The Dirtmeister®, and his sidekick Digger as your guides! From steaming, creeping lava, ground-shaking earthquakes, and incredible ice sheets to rocks, minerals, meteors, glaciers, fossils, soil, and more, you'll get the dirt on all the amazing geological processes at play on our planet every day.

DO YOU DIG ADVENTURE?

COOL CARTOONS   FUN FACT NUGGETS
SOLID SCIENCE   DO-IT-YOURSELF EXPERIMENTS